Psychological Survival

Stanley Cohen and Laurie Taylor

PSYCHOLOGICAL SURVIVAL

The Experience of Long-Term Imprisonment

 VINTAGE BOOKS

A Division of Random House, New York

FIRST VINTAGE BOOKS EDITION, March 1974

Copyright © 1972 by Stanley Cohen and Laurie Taylor
All rights reserved under International and Pan-American
Copyright Conventions. Published in the United States by
Random House, Inc., New York. Originally published in
England by Penguin Books Ltd., and in the United States
by Pantheon Books, a division of Random House, Inc., in
1972.

Library of Congress Cataloging in Publication Data

Cohen, Stanley.

  Psychological survival.

  Bibliography: p.
  1. Prison psychology. I. Taylor, Laurie,
1935–   joint author. II. Title.
[HV6089.C64 1974]   365'.6'019   73–13802
ISBN 0–394–71972–7

Manufactured in the United States of America

Contents

Preface		5
Chapter One	Getting into a maximum security wing	11
Chapter Two	Survival in extreme situations	41
Chapter Three	The closed emotional world of the security wing	60
Chapter Four	Time and deterioration	86
Chapter Five	History, authority and solidarity	112
Chapter Six	Making out and fighting back	129
Chapter Seven	Identities, biographies and ideologies	147
Chapter Eight	Taking sides	180
Appendix	The story of another research project	201
Selected Bibliography		209
About the Authors		219

Preface

All over the world there are hundreds of thousands of people in prisons, jails, labour camps and similar institutions. They are there to protect society from their actions and thoughts, to deter them and others from similar offences, to be punished by enforced seclusion and deprivation, to be persuaded or forced to conform, or simply to be put out of circulation. Where there is no death penalty, banishment or physical torture, to lock a person away for life or a long period of his life is the most severe form of punishment which a society uses. In this country some 40,000 prisoners are incarcerated. Some of these are destined to spend a very long time indeed in the same circumstances. A few will die in prison.

By chance, we became acquainted some four years ago with one small group of long-term prisoners in England, those locked up in the maximum security block – 'E-Wing' – of Durham Prison. In ways which we shall describe, we gradually became involved with them in a collaborative research project. This was at first largely concerned with penal policy and with orthodox criminological discussions about prison but we gradually found that the most viable way to make sense of our observations, was to understand E-Wing as a particular extreme situation and to interpret the men's behaviour as attempts to survive in this situation. Our first two chapters describe the setting up of this unique environment, our own entry into it and its resemblance to other extreme situations which make severe demands on the individual's ability to keep himself psychologically alive. The rest of the book depicts the problem of such survival.

The men we knew in E-Wing not only supported our plans to write up the research but some of them took the initiative in suggesting it in the first place. This does not mean that we always followed the directions they suggested, but we trust that they will understand our personal obsessions. If this book has any authenticity, it will be determined by their response to it. So although the objects of social scientific inquiry are rarely willing recipients of the attention bestowed upon them, in the case of the research reported here, there was at least some willingness among our 'subjects'. They respected our hope that this book, which concentrates on how people survive in extreme and adverse situations, would become a manual – a handbook for psychological survival – for others who find themselves in similar circumstances.

Almost all our material is from Durham and the prisons to which the E-Wing men were transferred. We were able, however, to supplement some of this with 'harder' data derived from an interview schedule designed and administered towards the end of 1971 by a different group of long-term prisoners in a prison which we call 'Eccleston'. A sample of just over 100 prisoners answered these questions and whenever we use these findings in the text we will refer simply to the 'Eccleston sample'. We are most grateful to all these men, and especially to two whom we cannot name, for all their help.

Our major debt, of course, is to the prisoners of E-Wing who appear under pseudonyms throughout this book. But we have, over the last four years, also received general encouragement and help on specific matters from many other people. We would like to mention all our friends and colleagues in the National Deviancy Conference; Ros Kane from Radical Alternatives to Prison; Jill Norman; David Woodhill; Marty Miller; Jason Ditton; Mark Beeson; and all the ex-E-Wing teachers, especially John Smith, Ian Taylor, Paul Walton and Simon Maddison; the prisoners' wives and friends whom we knew and others who will understand why we did not mention their names. Parts or the whole of an earlier draft were read by Bruce Jackson, Sheldon Messinger and Howard Becker and we are grateful to them for their comments.

We thank Margaret Silcock and Diana Strickland for all their help in putting the manuscript together; and Paul Barker, Editor of *New Society*, and Paul Atkinson of *New Edinburgh Review* for permission to use some of the material in Chapters Three and Four which originally appeared in somewhat different forms in their journals.

Finally, our thanks to Ruth Cohen and Kate Williams for contributing so significantly to the interpretation of our experiences over these years.

The old doctor felt my pulse, evidently thinking of something else the while. 'Good, good for there,' he mumbled, and then with a certain eagerness asked me whether I would let him measure my head. Rather surprised, I said Yes, when he produced a thing like calipers and got the dimensions back and front and every way, taking notes carefully . . . I thought him a harmless fool. 'I always ask leave, in the interests of science, to measure the crania of those going out there,' he said. 'And when they come back, too?' I asked. 'Oh, I never see them,' he remarked; 'and, moreover, the changes take place inside, you know.' He smiled, as if at some quiet joke.

Joseph Conrad, *The Heart of Darkness*

Psychological Survival

CHAPTER ONE

Getting into a maximum security wing

'It seems that they want to live like landed gentry.
They seem to be forgetting completely that they are
in prison for punishment.'
Durham Prison Officer, March 1968

In November 1967 we accepted an invitation from Durham
University Extra-Mural Department to give a short series of
weekly classes in social science to the long-term prisoners contained in 'E-Wing', the maximum security wing of Durham
prison. This was an important innovation. Classes of this sort
had not been tried in other security wings before and it was
nearly two years before moves were made to try the same sort
of thing at Parkhurst and Leicester, the sites of the other two
main security wings in this country. Anything which affected
life in these wings in any way was always viewed with great
suspicion and concern by prison officers, governors and the
Home Office.

Controversy had surrounded the wings as a whole (and
Durham wing in particular) since their foundation in 1964.
Durham itself was closed in June 1971 and we can now recount
something like its complete history. We are indulging in this
somewhat journalistic exercise not simply because of the story's
intrinsic appeal – although it has always had that for the media
and the public – but also because the events and policies we
describe had considerable private significance for the prisoners
themselves. This significance will be brought out in later
chapters; here we are simply setting the scene.

The Early History of the wing

The first suggestion that special security wings might be created in Britain came at the time of the train robbers' trial in 1963. Durham almost inevitably was amongst the three chosen locations. The main prison there already contained a special wing which had been set up after a series of escapes in 1961 as a special security and punishment block for noted and persistent escapers. It had thus acquired a reputation for impregnability, but this was not apparently its only characteristic. Several prisoners from the wing asked to give evidence of brutality by prison officers to a 1963 inquiry into allegations of ill-treatment of prisoners in Durham.[1] But as the report only concerned itself with ill-treatment in the main prison they were denied a hearing. The inquiry which rejected most of the allegations nevertheless revealed a considerable toleration of violence and neglect within the main prison. Conditions in the security wing which was semi-officially regarded as a 'punishment block' were, according to the later reports of inmates, even worse. One man talked of the 'terrible beatings' which were handed out by 'screws' who appeared to have been specially selected for their toughness.[2] Indeed, E-Wing was regarded for many years as a place in which prisoners were 'broken'. Of course one always has to rely upon inmate reports to make such evaluations but the consistency with which these have been made coupled with the general recognitions of major improvements in the wing after the series of disturbances in 1967 and 1968 suggest their reliability.

By 1965 the wing had been converted for the arrival of the train robbers, Goody, James and Field. The conversion was in

1. *Inquiry Held By the Visiting Committee into Allegations of Ill-treatment of Prisoners in Her Majesty's Prison, Durham* (Cmnd. 2068, June 1963).

2. We are aware that 'screw' is often a term of contempt which most prison officers do not like, but the word is so often used – by prisoners and very often by staff as well – that we have not sought for an alternative in this text, or placed the word in protective inverted commas.

response to the feeling that new ways of dealing with dangerous prisoners were now needed. The media and the judiciary made great play with the idea of a 'new' type of criminal who was more ruthless, more violent and more organized than his predecessors. The new security measures introduced during 1965 to help contain such men included electronic surveillance, dog runs, armed guards, gas masks, and (according to one report) the siting of a machine-gun nest on the external wall. Even these measures did not seem enough to reassure those worried about the escape of Ronald Biggs (another train robber) and others from Wandsworth in July of that year, for in November of 1965 troops were called in to guard the train robbers in Durham. This paranoid escalation was crowned by the Chief Constable of Durham early that year when he observed to a press conference:

I am satisfied that Goody's friends were prepared to launch something in the nature of a full-scale military attack, even to the extent of using tanks, bombs and what the Army describes as limited atomic weapons. Once armoured vehicles had breached the main gates there would be nothing to stop them. A couple of tanks could easily have come through the streets of Durham unchallenged. Nothing is too extravagant.

Apparently nothing was, for the Chief Constable's statement, which he later claimed was a deliberate diversionary tactic to cover the secret transfer of three prisoners to Parkhurst, was given national and credulous coverage. Meanwhile within the wing the inmates faced up to their special security treatment. The environment had been electrified for their arrival. The handles on the doors became 'live' even to fingertip touch once the electronic robot controls were switched on at night by prison officers, now nicknamed 'Daleks' because of their new-found automatism. The wing had closed circuit television to aid the monitoring of the prisoners and a specially trained officer sat in a bullet-proof steel and glass cubicle watching over the controls of this and other electronic devices. Subdued light burned all night in the train robbers' cells and at least one of them was forced to sleep with a handkerchief over his eyes. Over the coming years there were numerous permutations in the security arrangements involving dogs, extra electronic devices and the photographing of relatives to prevent impersonation. Concessions were eventually made over such matters as TV, radio, cooking facilities. The troops were withdrawn and the lights switched off at night, but the fundamental notion of a segregated maximum security unit remained.

The Introduction of Category A

The special status of the wings was formalized by the categorization policy recommended by the Mountbatten Report.[3] Following the escape of George Blake from Wormwood Scrubs in October 1966, the Home Secretary appointed Lord Mountbatten to inquire into prison escapes and security. The escape of a master spy and the status of the admiral was melodramatic enough, but in case the report required an additional twist, eight days before its publication, Frank Mitchell, the 'Mad Axeman', absconded from a Dartmoor working party.

Mountbatten made a number of recommendations about the security weaknesses he found; one was that prisoners should be divided into four main categories according to their security risk. Category A prisoners should be those 'whose escape would be highly dangerous to the public or the police or to the security of the State'. In 1967 the Prison Department compiled a list of 138 convicted prisoners in this category. They were all serving long sentences for serious offences: only five out of this number were serving periods of less than 10 years, forty were serving periods of 14 years and over, and forty-eight were doing life sentences (see Tables I and II). It was only men from this category who made up the population of the wings after this date and it was only these men whom we got to know. (The number of Category A men is now just over 200.)

High security prisoners and long-termers are not exactly the

3. *Report of the Inquiry into Prison Escapes and Security* (Cmnd. 3175, 1966).

same groups and the original 138 Category A men were to form part of an increasing number of prisoners serving very long sentences.

TABLE I

Records of 138 Category A prisoners. List of the main charges of which the prisoner was found guilty on the occasion of his most recent conviction.

Murder or manslaughter	47
Robbery with violence	42
Other offences of violence (grievous bodily harm, wounding, attempted murder)	22
Heterosexual assaults	7
Homosexual assaults	2
Breaking in	7
Official Secrets Act	6
Receiving	2
Possession of firearms	1
Arson	1
Attempted escape	1
	138

In 1970 the prisons contained 225 men serving sentences of exactly ten years, 218 serving over ten years and 159 serving 'life'. 'Life' used to mean an average of nine years; longer periods were very unusual. However, with the abolition of capital punishment, many lifers will now, in the words of the 1968 Home Office report, 'have to be detained for a very much longer than average period'. In fact at the end of 1968 the number of life sentence prisoners who had served over nine years was forty-seven, at the end of 1969 it was fifty-nine, by the end of 1970 it was seventy-one, and by the end of 1971 it had increased to eighty-five of whom sixteen had served more than 13 years. The probability of 'life' meaning more than nine years has been formalized by the increasing tendency of judges to incorporate in their sentences 'recommendations' for a minimum term of anything up to thirty years; the cases of Harry Roberts, the Kray brothers, and Joseph Sewell are well-known examples.

In October 1971 Mr Justice Chapman sentencing two men to life imprisonment for murdering a police detective recommended that one should be kept for twenty-five years and the other till he died: 'My recommendation to the Home Secretary will be that those dreadful words I have just used should have their awful, dreadful meaning. In other words, life should mean life.' This was the first time that a judge had officially recommended that a man be held in prison for the remainder of his

TABLE II

Records of 138 Category A Prisoners
Total length of the sentences currently being served

Total Length of Sentence (Years)	Number of Inmates
4	1
5	1
6	1
8	2
10	26
10½	1
11¼	1
11½	1
12	14
13	2
14	8
15	12
16	2
17	4
18	3
19	1
20	2
21	1
22	1
23	1
30	5
Life	48
Total	138

Tables I and II are taken from 'The Régime for Long-Term Prisoners in Conditions of Maximum Security', *Report of the Advisory Council on the Penal System.* HMSO 1968, pp. 90 and 91. (*The Radzinowicz Report*)

life. Such recommendations are not, in the words of the Home Secretary, 'binding' but they 'will be given the fullest weight'.

At the same time, *fixed* sentences of over 14 years are increasing (for example, the train robbers, the Richardson gang, John MacVicar); and in the four years, 1964–8, fifty-one men were sentenced to over 14 years. This total includes seven sentences of 21–5 years and another seven of 30. In the unlikely event of these men gaining maximum remission, they will have to serve at least 14 years.

All this means that our prisons now contain far more than the 'handful' of prisoners which the Home Office described as serving over 15 years in the 1968 report. This also means – as the Prison Officers Association in particular has taken pains to point out – that there will be more men in the prisons whose 'nothing to lose' attitude will render them continual escape risks and sources of trouble and violence.

The Later History: after the Admiral

It was principally in 1966 that Durham's security wing came into the public eye. There was the bizarre atomic weapons episode and then, at the end of the year, a phrase in the Mountbatten report which condemned the conditions in all the wings 'as such no country with a record for civilized behaviour ought to tolerate any longer than is absolutely necessary as a stop-gap measure'. Despite the Admiral of the Fleet's comments and their reiteration two years later in the Radzinowicz Report it took over four years before E-Wing was closed and a new policy announced – but not yet implemented – for security prisoners.[4]

The later history of the wing was full of excitement, if not

4. The special security wings are to be phased out – Durham has been the first and, so far, the only one to go – and Category A prisoners will be dispersed to a number of selected prisons. By the end of 1971 some twenty-five Category A prisoners were still in the special wings at Chelmsford, Leicester and Parkhurst. The Home Office's affection for Durham's E-Wing lingers on, and a redecorated and apparently renamed version, will shortly be opened for 'medium- to long-termers'.

for its occupants at least for the mass media. The wing was seldom out of the news: there were hunger strikes, escape bids, secret transfers, disturbances, protests and a dramatic escape at the end of 1968. An exclusive club, with its own tie, was formed by those journalists who had a steady line in E-Wing stories. The public's interest in these stories was heightened by the notoriety of their participants. The wing had contained during these years Charles and Eddie Richardson, Ronald Kray and other members of his 'Firm', the Shepherds Bush police killers, David Burgess, most of the train robbers (Reynolds, Goody, Wisbey), Dennis Stafford, Ian Brady, Raymond Morris, Walter Probyn and (for a shorter time than planned) John MacVicar.

Besides the 1968 escape, the most dramatic events of the wing's history were two disturbances at the beginning of 1967 and the beginning of 1968. We will describe these in some detail, for they were, despite their atypical nature, the events which coloured both public and inmate attitudes to the wings. The behaviour of prisoners, prison officers, press and Home Office during these disturbances reveals the stereotypes which pervade the prison system with more clarity than does a day-to-day discussion of prison routine.

The 1967 Football Mutiny

All through 1966 security measures were intensified in the wing. The atomic weapon episode of February, far from sounding like an over-reaction, seemed to give fresh ingenuity to those determined to make Durham totally impregnable. This ingenuity was finally blessed by the Mountbatten recommendations on security which were implemented with indecent haste at Durham as elsewhere in the system. Not that there was much room for tightening up in E-Wing itself: there were already complaints about exercise, overcrowding (at the beginning of 1967 there were about fifty men in the wing, the highest number it was ever to hold), visiting facilities (a small room with husband and wife sitting at opposite ends of a table, having to shout at each other to be heard while a prison officer listened) and working conditions (most men had done nothing but sew mail bags for the past eighteen months). In the middle of January two of the men's wives had warned the Home Office that incidents would take place unless conditions were improved; they had been worried by the signs of mental and physical stress they had seen in their husbands. One long-termer (who recently died in prison) specifically told his wife that the atmosphere was such that trouble could be expected. Later in that month twenty-one of the E-Wing prisoners listed fifty complaints to the Visiting Committee. These were all found to be groundless, although a concession was made in allowing one man to play a guitar in his cell.

At 1.00 a.m. on 9 February the police were tipped off that there was to be a break from E-Wing and the city was immediately sealed off by a police road block till early in the morning. But there was no break and the real story – which did not reach the press for two days – had happened on the Thursday (8 February).

About ten or eleven prisoners had been playing soccer in the exercise yard and the ball was kicked into the barbed wire circling the yard. One of the three prison officers on guard refused them permission to retrieve it (on the grounds, apparently, that this might be a ruse for a mass breakout) but the men started to form a pyramid to recover the ball. The officer tried to stop them, had his cap knocked off and one of the prisoners spat in his eye. The men started running back to their cells and at some time in the next two hours decided to make some mass protest. This erupted at 7.00 p.m. Although a core of fifteen originally started the disturbance, some thirty-five eventually took part. For about five hours mugs, dishes and burning pieces of linen were thrown onto the screws in the yard below. This was the point at which the Governor called the police and the city was encircled.

Eventually four men barricaded themselves in their cells and were soon joined by seven others. Broken furniture was wedged against the cell doors and material stuffed in the keyholes to prevent the screws from peering in. There was much noise and shouting and the whole wing was surrounded by officers keeping up a barrage of threats about what they would do to the men. This lasted for nearly three days. What happened next is a matter of disagreement between the prison authorities and the prisoners. We have talked to some of the men who were observing the events from their cells. On the basis of criteria such as internal consistency in these and other accounts we are of the opinion that their versions of what happened are substantially correct. We reproduce below edited versions of just two accounts of these events, derived mainly from letters smuggled out of Parkhurst Prison in April 1971 and given publicity by the National Organization for the Defence of Prisoners and Dependants (N.O.D.P.D.).[5]

1) 'I was kept in solitary on Rule 43 until I was sent to Durham security wing some months later. It was here that I was to see two of the worst beatings I have ever seen. This was the result of an incident which arose through conditions in the wing: not only did they (the prison staff) treat us like animals, but did themselves act like animals.

'On the night in question about ten of us decided we had to draw attention to conditions in the wing, so it was decided that we would barricade ourselves in our cells and refuse to come out.

'We thought that if we could get a bit of publicity conditions would change for the better. Little did we expect the violence that was to follow as a result of us barricading ourselves in our cells.

'In the early hours of the morning prison officers accompanied by the Prison Governor and Works Prison Officer entered the wing. Everybody knew the screws' blood was up, for they were screaming and shouting what they were going to do to us. Still I thought we were pretty safe as they could not get in our cells. Later works screws arrived with crowbars and a sledgehammer and went to Marty's door. One Prison Officer called Marty to come out. I presume Marty came to the door, for another big screw jabbed through his spy hole with a large crowbar (at this

5. These were reproduced in various forms in INK (26.6.71) and (3.7.71) and *Irish Liberation Press* (7.6.71). The names quoted in the original have been changed.

stage most of us had smashed out our spy holes and holder leaving a sizeable hole about the size of a fist or bigger). Marty's door was eventually broken down and he was given a severe beating. He struck back at them — there were six or seven of them – and he was laid out on the landing where they continued to beat him with riot sticks, and a P.O. was striking him about the body with a jemmy. Two P.O.s laid into Marty with sticks, as did some others whom I did not know. Personally I say Marty was fortunate that the screws got in each other's way and could not get the full swing of their sticks on the narrow landing. Unlike Marty, William was taken from the security wing to the main prison. I was called to the window by another prisoner, and I could see a man being dragged by the arms up the hill to the main wing, where he was being beaten and kicked by screws on either side of him. I was later to learn that this had been William. May I quote that William was known by the prison staff to suffer from blackouts and dizzy spells, yet he was beaten up with no thought of this whatsoever. Both Marty and William could have been killed that night.' —

2) 'I am a prisoner serving a life sentence. In February 1967 I was a prisoner in the Durham maximum security wing. I along with fourteen other long-term prisoners agreed to barricade myself in my cell as a way of protesting against the conditions in the security wing . . . We had used all of the normal channels. . . . the Home Office, the Board of Visiting Committee were seen, a prison director was seen and letters sent to our various members of Parliament, all to no avail.

'The conditions we complained about were visits, work, exercise, food, no association, attitude of staff, rigid discipline. When we had a visit from our wives and children we were not allowed any physical contact; we could not hold our children or kiss them . . .'

The police were brought in to help the warders and after three days barricaded in his cell, during which time this man was given no food or water whatsoever,

'. —. the staff started to force my door down. When the door did come down I was dragged outside onto the landing . . . I was thrown down a flight of stairs where other officers held my arms and legs whilst another kicked me in my testicles; my legs were wide apart and I couldn't cover myself in any way. I was being beaten with riot sticks at the same time until I went into a semi-conscious state. I was dragged along the floor into a strong room. This is a concrete cell with a wooden board for a bed. My clothing was ripped from my body forcibly. I kicked out as much as possible hitting one of the officers on the leg. A principal officer shouted "Break his legs." My legs were placed across the wooden board and were repeatedly beaten with riot sticks until I lost consciousness. When I recovered I was beaten unconscious again. This went on over a period of hours. Some time later a doctor came into the room and stitched my wounds. My face and body were one mass of bruises. I was unable to use my hands for seven days.

'I wasn't given any food for three days and when I was the soup had urine in it and the meal phlegm on top of it. When I complained to the Governor, he said "It was my imagination, and if I didn't like it I didn't have to eat it." I remained in the strong box for twenty-three days ... Later I was charged with gross personal violence against a Prison Officer. I believe this was only done to cover the brutality that had been committed on me. I was put before a visiting magistrate and given the maximum sentence. I complained to the Board over the brutality that had been used on me. The magistrate dismissed my complaint saying: "You have been in rough houses before so what can you expect." '

It was clear even from the initials press reports that – whatever else had happened – there had been a great deal of violence. There were early reports that one prisoner had received fourteen stitches in a head wound and that others had been injured when the officers stormed the barricades. It was reported that one prisoner was badly hurt when falling accidentally down the steps of the wing. The Home Office stated that these injuries were relatively minor. One Prison Officer was reported as being hurt. There were few details about how the barricade ended, except a terse statement that hand-picked officers had entered the cells, armed with batons and shielded with mattresses and that the prisoners concerned had been placed on solitary confinement.

Various public allegations of brutality were made which the

P.O.s at Durham took seriously enough to announce their intention of being represented at the hearing of the charges against the four prisoners singled out for their part in the disturbances. In the next week various groups, including the N.C.C.L., ex-prisoners and the wives of some of the prisoners called for an inquiry. Meantime in the prison, the Governor (after police tip-offs) warned some staff that there might be a danger of reprisals. It was suggested that London groups with north-east connections might take revenge on the screws involved in the barricade.

About three weeks after the disturbances the press announced that '17 Durham Jail rebels pay penalty'; five were dealt with by the Visiting Committee, twelve by the Governor. The sentences (for offences including assault, damaging prison property and refusing to obey orders) ranged from forfeiture of remission of up to thirty days (for the lifers) to restricted diet (R.D.) and loss of privileges for up to fifty-six days. (R.D. meant bread and water two out of three days, loss of privileges, no smoking, T.V., or association.)

Clearly the events worried the Home Office. At the beginning of April it was announced that an inquiry was to be held, run by north-eastern magistrates and a Home Office official. The team was to spend three days investigating the brutality allegations and the general charges.

The inquiry started taking statements from various persons involved in the incident, and a few ex-prisoners who had been in Durham. One of the E-Wing men, Louis, shouted as he left the inquiry: 'We were massacred.' In the next month or so there were odd leaks about the report in the press and in the wing itself and some speculation as to whether or not it would be published. None of these leaks was particularly reassuring. On 1 May Mr Percy, the Chairman of the Visiting Magistrates' Committee was quoted as saying:

Some prisoners have small complaints from time to time. These are sometimes trivial and forgotten. The prisoner, however, watches to see what action is taken and if he sees none, he thinks he has been forgotten. I know these fellows think that nobody cares about them, but I hope they think they have had a fair hearing.

A week later the press leaked a story that the Report had cleared the P.O.s of any brutality, and had found that although violence had been used in two cases on the instructions of the Governor, this was no more than was needed to maintain discipline. This leak produced the following reaction from Percy: 'There is a modicum of truth in it, but that is all. The disturbing feature about the leak is that prisoners have access to newspapers. If they see headlines like "Prison Officers Cleared" they won't like it one bit.'

Finally, a month later (23.6.67), the Home Secretary, Mr Jenkins, announced in the Commons that the Report showed no evidence of brutal treatment in the wing. Force had to be used against the three men who had evidently resisted removal from their cells. The committee reported a conflict of evidence on the men's allegations, found no evidence of ill-treatment before or after the incident and said that the eighteen prisoners involved had no knowledge of such treatment.

But the committee had noted that some conditions were unsatisfactory and these were now on the way to being improved. Their view was that the disturbances were not due to brutality but to tensions and conflicts which had built up and which were in large measure due to the unsatisfactory physical conditions which – according to the Home Secretary – were now being investigated. Apparently the committee had recommended that more privileges should be allowed. The only two concrete ones mentioned were plans to build workshops away from the cell blocks and to allow the prisoners to play cards together. 'There's no reason why four of them shouldn't sit down in a cell and have a game of cards. The security is good enough', Mr Percy was quoted as saying.

The 1968 Chapel Barricade

The early months of 1968 were ones of more than usual tension in the wing. The disgruntlement with the findings about the

1967 disturbances had by no means subsided and the improvements that had been made towards the end of the year had not satisfied anybody. For the last six months of that year the men had remained in their cells most of the day and there were no work opportunities at all. There had been constant complaints about the food and general conditions.

The Governor (now Mr Gordon Chambers, following the quiet transfer of Major Bride after his role in the earlier events) responded to the need for varying the routine in the wing by having two workshops constructed. One was for making ornamental metal, the other, a 'light textile shop', was fitted with sewing machines and the men were to make aprons, bags and mosquito nets. The new régime was to start on the first Monday of March and also entailed the men having to do their own domestic cleaning, previously done by first offenders from the main wing of the prison.

Neither of these innovations was particularly welcomed: the workshops because their introduction was seen as only a marginal concession (most of the men did not care for the work offered), and the new cleaning duties because this meant the loss of valuable outside contacts. In any event, all the cumulative grievances were focused on this issue and some of the men gave notice that they would refuse to cooperate on the opening date. When the Governor finally announced the details he was met by a chorus of catcalls from the men.

At about 8 p.m. on the night of 3 March, the day before the new plan was to start and almost exactly a year after the 'football mutiny', the trouble began. Obviously, something was expected: four hours earlier the Chairman of the Visiting Magistrates' Committee made a twenty-five mile journey to the prison, because – as he later told a credulous press – he 'thought something was going to happen'. In fact he had, along with many others, been told that negotiations had broken down in the prison and that the Assistant Governor had been warned by the prisoners' chief negotiator to expect trouble. Twenty-one prisoners broke out of their cells and, after overpowering a prison officer and taking his keys, barricaded themselves in the chapel and the A.G.'s office opposite this. (One of their first actions was to use the outside telephone in the A.G.'s office to contact the press and various friends.)

An emergency message for police reinforcements was sent out on the hot line to Durham division police H.Q. and within minutes the prison was surrounded and three van loads of police with dogs went inside the walls to take up positions in the prison yard. At about midnight a Home Office spokesman announced:

We are leaving them there for the night to cool down. Guards will remain on duty outside the chapel. We understand that the prisoners have certain grievances, nothing in particular. We do not know exactly what happened to the Prison Officer they over-powered. But he was not hurt and they did not barricade him in with them. The men would not be given food and drink, but had nothing happened, they would have got cocoa and biscuits as usual. What happens in the morning is up to the Governor.

One of the Governor's first actions was to order the heating and lighting to be cut off. The men settled in for the night.

Most press reports the next morning carried details and photos of the more notorious prisoners in the wing at the time and named two well-known criminals as the leaders in the 'audacious action'.

Then, in the words of Mr Thomas Percy, the Chairman of the Visiting Magistrates, a day later, 'This time we [sic] decided to let them sweat it out. We turned off the heat and lights and there were no toilets in the chapel. After the last trouble at Durham we thought we had settled the complaints. I don't think they have anything to complain about at the moment.'[6]

6. This was, of course, an extraordinary statement to be made by the Chairman of the Visiting Committee, a judicial body with fairly comprehensive functions and powers and supposedly independent of the prison administration. It was hardly calculated to give the prisoners much faith in the integrity of this body. One of us immediately wrote a letter to the local press, pointing out that:

'It would be natural to presume that some sort of disciplinary procedure will result from the disturbances in Durham and hence the

In the meantime, the men began fairly systematically to destroy the three rooms that made up their fortress: the A.G.'s office, the Senior Officer's room and the Chapel. The barricades were constructed with filing cabinets, tables and the altar and other fittings ripped out of the Chapel. Before the filing cabinets were used – and most of their contents destroyed – the men enjoyed some moments of grim delight reading their confidential files.

Some twenty-five hours after the barricades had been set up, the demonstration was over. Late on the Monday night, they 'surrendered' after about five minutes' talk with the Director of Prisons Administration, Alan Bainton (someone known and respected by many of the men). He apparently told them that they had 'put themselves in a stupid and ridiculous position' from which they had nothing to gain and after talking among themselves for about ten minutes, the men put the matter to the vote and decided to give up. A letter of negotiation was drafted by some of the men, demanding particularly a guarantee that no violent recrimination should take place against them.

There was, needless to say, little sympathy with the prisoners. The press took much delight in reporting their ignominious retreat from the barricades: they 'shuffled out' and were searched, given baths or showers, fed ('chops, roast potatoes and apple pie', as was reported to indicate how misguidedly soft the authorities were) and locked up in their cells.

Unlike the aftermath of the riot a year earlier, there were no violent attacks on the men by the staff. Apart from two periods

---

Chairman of the Visiting Committee is likely to be involved. As this body has a quasi-judicial function, the Chairman would seem to be disqualified from adjudicating if he has already prejudged the issue by firstly identifying with the actions taken by the prison administration and secondly stating that the prisoners have nothing to complain about.'

Through various bodies, we also raised the matter with the Home Office and Lord Chancellor and in the event Percy was 'advised to stand down' from the later inquiry, together with two other magistrates who were present during the barricade.

of exercise – half an hour in the morning and half an hour in the afternoon – the men involved were confined to their cells until the adjudicating authority was to hear the cases. The Home Secretary was pressed in the Commons about replacing the wings with a special security prison and the Shadow Home Secretary asked him to consider whether the Durham disturbance was partly due to the absence of such a maximum security prison. The Home Secretary replied that he was waiting for the findings of the Radzinowicz Report, due in the next few weeks.

The episode was written up – particularly by the local press – as 'Victory For the New Boy'. (Gordon Chambers: Governor of Trouble Torn Durham Prison, ex-army officer, one of the new breed of progressive prison chiefs, etc.) These write-ups made it clear that it was the Governor's progressive attitude, his desire to improve the monotony of the prison routine, that had led to the latest E-Wing explosion. The prisoners were described as a pampered élite, ungrateful for the concessions made to them; they had no cause for complaint and indeed their conditions were too soft. Universally, the 'aristocrats of E-Wing' were condemned. One Prison Officer told the press: 'It seems that they want to live like landed gentry. They seem to be forgetting completely that they are in prison for punishment.'

They were condemned for not having worked regularly for six months and details were also given of the privileges they had received after the 1967 mutiny: an officer regularly buying them titbits in the city's foodshops, 'fagging' by first offenders. Things had never been better in Durham since it was opened 159 years before with full solitary confinement and the treadmill. Perhaps in the interests of all, it would be better to go back to such a system.

Nothing as drastic as this resulted. After a long banning of facilities such as T.V., cookery, other classes and P.T., disciplinary hearings took place in front of the Visiting Magistrates' Committee. Twenty of the men were found guilty of mutiny, nineteen of these also of malicious damage. Their pay and canteen facilities were stopped for between twenty to fifty days and they were all ordered to be confined to their cells for forty-two days. A few days later, a demonstration took place against these sentences, in the form of about three quarters of an hour of shouting, chanting, banging utensils and kicking cell doors. This demonstration was left unpunished.

Over the next few months – in what one of the prisoners, Chris, referred to as 'the diaspora of Spring 1968' – many of the mutineers were quietly transferred to other prisons. The last three years of the wing saw a dramatic escape from the officially 'escape-proof' wing, when three men – one of whom was to remain uncaptured for nearly two years – climbed out through a ventilation shaft with an ingenuity which made many of the legendary war-time escapes look like Sunday afternoon jaunts from an open Borstal. There was also a series of peaceful protests about the visiting regulations and a number of lengthy hunger strikes by one particular prisoner, whose notoriety was sufficient to make his least action good material for the front pages of the tabloids. But the eventful times between 1967 and 1968 were not repeated. They remained only in the collective memories of all who passed through the wing. The solidarity of the men had brought about some general improvements. But there were still many private struggles to survive in the wing which had to be resolved in other ways.

Moving onto the Research

Given the history of the wing and its consequent notoriety, the nervousness of the Governor about our entering it at the end of 1967 was understandable. He cautiously suggested to us that we might 'talk on any topic at all provided it was not connected with the mens' lives' – an injunction which recalls Rule 5 of the educational notebook (No. 991) which is issued to prisoners: 'You may if you wish, take this book out with you when you are discharged provided that you have not (1) Written in it about any of the following matters: a) your own life.' The Governor's request was not easy to respect. Sociology and psychology despite their increasing enshrinement within academic institutions have a nasty habit of becoming relevant to people's lives and we gradually moved both in content and structure away from the night-school syndrome.

It was not only the Governor who expressed a certain anxiety about our entrance to the wing. Other Prison Officers clearly identified us with the general forces of permissiveness which they felt were eroding its true nature. Several press reports had given publicity to officers who felt the wing was not tough enough. At the end of 1966 some Prison Officers had described the long-termers as 'molly-coddled' and advocated an army 'glass house' model in order that they might be kept active. As evidence of softness they cited the painting of the interior of the building, the introduction of new lino and the 'waiter-service' which provided meals for high-risk men. The *Newcastle Journal* (7.3.67) recounted under the heading 'E-Wing warder quits' the story of an officer who claimed to have resigned because of 'the atmosphere, the approach by the Home Office and the snide remarks from the prisoners ... The standing of the Prison Officer is belittled.' He said some men from the south had an 'attitude of contempt for the Geordie screws'.

It was difficult not to be aware of staff resentment both inside and outside the prison. One night we were foolish enough to visit the officers' social club and there a senior officer happened to overhear our discussion about payment for the classes which was made by the Durham Extra-Mural Department. He butted into the conversation to observe in a friendly way that he was pleased we were being paid and 'not going in to talk to those animals for nothing'.

We first taught in a room on the ground floor and later moved to another small room on the first floor which, like every other part of the building, had a particular symbolic significance for the men: it had been converted from the chapel destroyed during the March 1968 barricade. Now it was used for classes and making soft toys.

When the class first started an officer sat outside the door, his presence interpreted by us as either a reassurance that help would be on hand if the men were to attack us or as a method by which the authorities could keep a check on the content of our discussions. The latter reason seemed more real to us, although the idea that the men might hold us as hostages was seriously posed by the authorities at one time and jokingly referred to by the men on a few occasions.

The possibility of censorship was removed when eventually the officer gave up his vigil outside the door. The men also assured us that the room was not bugged. For a few months during alterations to the wing, the class moved to a room without a door. The men responded by placing a blackboard across the entrance, shutting out at least the sight of the three or four officers sitting on the landing a few feet away. The absence of doors was not unusual in the wing: most daily routines, including going to the lavatory, were open to official surveillance.

The classes averaged two and a half hours in length and sometimes when they ran over the prescribed limits an officer would come to the door and remind us of the time. A ceremonial part of the class, never once missed out, was the serving of tea by an old offender who had done about fifteen years inside and whom the men had good-naturedly adopted as a mascot despite the nature of his conviction which would normally have imposed at least partial ostracism upon him.

The class itself, although attendance was voluntary, became part of the natural time scheduling in the wing. It varied in size between two and twelve depending on transfers to other wings and the men's interest in the subject. At one time or another some fifty men passed through the class. Of these we got to know about ten intimately and an equal number fairly well. The class started at 6 p.m. – just after the evening meal – and finished only a short time before lights out at 9.00. As such it had to compete with television viewing. (We sometimes felt peculiarly flattered when members of one of the country's most notorious gangs preferred to attend our classes on sociology rather than watch 'The Untouchables'.)

The research which is described in this book was initiated in these classes during the early months of 1968. We had begun to move away from formal sociology towards unprogrammed discussions and it was during these that general criticism of traditional prison studies was voiced. We agreed with the prisoners in their feelings that many such studies failed to do justice to the full psychological effects of imprisonment by concentrating upon the prison as a social system or by merely describing the typical roles played in the prison community. If these aspects of the prison were put on one side, then one could see that the psychological problems posed for men in prisons had affinities with those which occurred in other extreme environments; they could be seen as arising from disturbances in the basic routines and assumptions which informed everyday life in more normal circumstances.

At this point the idea of a mutual research project was discussed. Initially, we saw ourselves as adding something to the current policy debates about security and long-term imprisonment and this, we think, was the men's main interest. We have on occasions provided evidence to various organizations, such as the Penal Affairs Committee of the Society of Friends, and R.A.P. (Radical Alternatives to Prison), but it became clear as the research developed that all of us wanted to go further than merely discussing the relative merits of such matters as whether to concentrate security risks in an Alcatraz-like prison or to disperse them in a number of units throughout the system.

The 'emergence' of our research at least allowed us to escape from the chronological lie which is at the heart of most research. Academic journals are full of studies which follow a fixed sequence of aims, methods, presentation of results and finally the 'discussions' or 'conclusion'. The social scientist according to this account of research sits at home pondering a problem, has a 'eureka' experience, rushes out armed with appropriate tests, applies them to the reality outside and then comes back indoors to resume a reflective stance. But as we have already indicated we started without a problem, evolved a set of methods while we worked, and ended up with a collection of observations, anecdotes, and descriptions rather than a table of results. Even the subjects of our research had the habit of becoming researchers in their own right so that at times we have been uncertain of the distinction between observer and observed. Rather like the tourists who went by coach to visit the hippies in Haight–Ashbury, we have felt ourselves to be doing no more than gazing at our own images in mirrors held up by our intended subjects.

For long periods of time we have probably talked more intimately to these men than to any other people we know. Our identification with them was enhanced by our inability completely to reject their view of the screws who they claimed were 'thick' and insensitive. The staff's suspicion that we were 'in league' with the men had therefore some basis. Certainly we have detected an odd reciprocal granting of élite status between us and them. We are university teachers, they are Category A prisoners. Outside on the landing sit the plebs.

However, the situation was more ambiguous than this. While there might be certain identifications between us and the prisoners, there are also many areas of disjunction. It was initially not very easy, for example, to feel relaxed in a room which contained a number of supposedly dangerous and volatile criminals. We were rarely conscious of any danger – although the prisoners correctly sensed that one of our colleagues was so nervous during the lecture period that he failed to appear for his subsequent classes. As one member remarked, 'How does it feel teaching people you've read so much about?' At that stage we were at least able to shelter behind our formal lecturing role, but sudden moments of self-consciousness occurred: thus, in hunting for an illustration of a point relating to psychological 'abnormality', we might cite an offender not in the room, but who was in the same wing and who belonged to the same gang as one of those present. We felt on those occasions the class enjoyed our embarrassment. They were able to gain social advantages from wearing their public images in a bland way. These men had a very good idea of such public definitions. During the 1968 chapel riot they had read the reports of themselves written by governors, probation officers, chaplains and all the other agents of social control who had stood like mile-stones marking out most of their adult life.

They consciously enjoyed their public reputation at times; we both recall the frisson which we felt when one of the gang members in what was almost an aside said 'of course, I'm a murderer' in much the same way that he might have said he was an engineer. On another occasion one of the men remarked in the course of an argument that he was the only one in the room who wasn't a murderer; apart from us there were seven people present in the room. On most occasions though, past convictions were hardly salient at all, and the men neither on their own nor in the class spent much time on such subjects.

We would not now expect murderers to exhibit especial aggression, nor train robbers to show excessive guile. As our belief in the stereotypes diminished, so our knowledge of the actual careers of the men became less critical. Concomitantly, our embarrassment in the situation decreased, and their hold over us by their ability to induce such embarrassment was similarly attenuated. However, we still make serious gaffes. Recently one of us was discussing spies in an atmosphere still charged with the adventures of Biggs in Australia. In the presence of another train robber we asked, in a discussion about Kim Philby, how a man could live for any period of time in an alien environment without arousing suspicion. The silence indicated that we had gone too far. This had begun to sound like a request for information. We apologized, admitted our embarrassment and changed the subject.

We believe that the prisoners trusted us throughout the research. At first they thought we were there to get information about escapes or attitudes to authority, but they gradually accepted our assurances about confidentiality (although, as they often observed, we could have been cleverer agents of social control than they had encountered before). All we can do is to go on talking as honestly as we can about our role, and hope that time, and indeed this book, will provide the type of confirmation they required.

Research Methods

Given the subtle social situation that we have described, it was obviously not possible to turn up one evening with a set of questionnaires for the men to complete. In the circumstances it would have been difficult to ask the prisoners to complete forms which were designed to turn them into special kinds of people – into extroverts, psychopaths or high achievers. In any case the standard tests were known to the men who frequently told stories about fiddling this or that test in order to achieve particular concessions in the prison. One of them described in detail how to fill in one personality test in such a way as to ensure that he was given outside work during the summer. Not that standard personality inventories are very appropriate for long-term prison populations. There's not much point in asking a man who's been inside for ten years and faces another twenty, whether or not he can 'easily get some life into a rather dull party' (to quote item 51 of the widely used Eysenck Personality Inventory).

Neither did the structured interview seem initially appropriate. The construction of categories implied by this method rests on the assumption that the interviewer knows enough about the socio-cultural world of the subject to tap meaningful areas. We still felt ourselves to be in a position of cultural map-makers who had as yet found only a few shifting landmarks. The men knew much more about the territory than we did and to constrain them within our categories would have been presumptuous at that stage.

We relied instead upon four major research methods. Firstly, we used unstructured group interviews at various stages of the research, often as ways of summarizing attitudes to particular areas. After extensive discussion for example, we would reach a point where individuals were anxious to formulate their overall feelings, either collectively or privately. We would record our observations and interpretations and then if possible, show these to the men. Secondly, we made extensive use of the men's writing. Even while we were visiting them in the wing we also maintained contact by letter, so that they might have a chance to produce written as well as verbal impressions. This correspondence has been maintained (precariously, because of Home Office censorship) now that the wing has closed and we continue to contact all previous members of the class. In addition to letters, the men have produced stories, essays and poems relating to their circumstances. Some of this work is quoted explicitly in the following pages but more often, as with interview material, we have incorporated the ideas into the general text.

During the course of our visits the men were consistently asking for literature which touched on aspects of their own lives; they were interested in novels and plays which dealt with such subjects as imprisonment, sexual deprivation, mysticism, anarchism, murder.[7] This enabled us to use literary identification as a third way for discovering opinions. This method would typically follow a pattern. A particular problem – say masturbation – might be concentrated upon in a discussion of Freud. This would lead easily into a general discussion of masturbation, in which techniques, fears and notable performances would be discussed. The actual feelings of the men about the subject could however then be further elaborated by reference for example to Genet's *Our Lady of the Flowers* or Roth's *Portnoy's Complaint*. This would enable them to select one or other literary contribution as most accurate or honest and thus provide us with a more sensitive indication of the significance of the behaviour than would have been obtained from a general discussion of a topic such as masturbation which raises certain defensive attitudes. This does not mean that literary contributions were always related to the men's actual behaviour. When we discussed different accounts of murder for example, we asked 'Could that have been the way Mersault (in Camus's *Outsider*) or Raskolnikov (in Dostoyevsky's *Crime*

7. The men only saw this material because of an oversight in the otherwise stringent security measures which allowed us to take it into the wing with us. Attempts to send such material through the normal channels have not always been successful.

and Punishment) felt?' rather than 'Did *you* feel like that when you murdered?' This method was particularly useful when applied to prison material. It enabled the men to make fine distinctions between different accounts of particular problems, which would not have been possible without some type of 'projective' material. We found, for example, that Victor Serge's account of types of adaptation to prison life which was written at the beginning of this century had more truth for these men than many contemporary literary or sociological accounts.

This method has been attacked by some critics on the grounds that it consists of putting 'words into people's mouths'. But any invitation to provide an opinion or attitude involves structuring the reply in certain ways. Questionnaires not only provide inflexible questions but restrict answers by insisting upon choice amongst pre-arranged responses or by imposing limits upon the amount of space and time which are taken up in replying. The psychoanalyst or the social worker who seeks opinions and attitudes from his clients does not do so without having a predetermined idea of which replies deserve most attention. At least we provided a number of interpretations and asked the men to identify themselves with one from this selection.

Our final research method was simply the writing up of the research. The papers that we have produced so far have been read and corrected by the men. They object if our language becomes too sociological, or our prose too academic. They affirm the integrity of the responses to the environment we describe and suggest ways in which the problems can be illustrated. This does not mean that they are totally responsible for all the faults of style and description in this book. They are far too polite to go on criticizing us beyond a certain point and we are allowed a certain degree of sociologizing in view of the academic nature of our reference groups.

These research methods were not chosen by default. They were the best ways that we knew to obtain a phenomenological picture of life in E-Wing for maximum security prisoners. We are pleased that our work meets the hopes expressed by the 1968 Home Office report, *The Régime of Long-Term Prisoners in Conditions of Maximum Security* which said 'It is too easy to talk about research "on" prisoners without realizing the great value of research "with" prisoners.' We have felt a little sad at times that the meaning of this phrase appears to have been withheld from those officials at the Home Office who have dealt with our subsequent applications for research facilities.[8]

The chronicle of our relationships with the Home Office is not encouraging to anyone concerned with the general future of prison research in this country. From our own point of view, though, our good fortune in getting into the prison the way we did, meant that we were able to bypass if not solve some of the problems of access, sponsorship and organization endemic to all social research and which are particularly acute in research on deviance. Institutionalized deviants are the 'property' of government agencies like the Home Office and most research on these populations is sponsored by such agencies and governed by regulations such as the Official Secrets Act.

This puts certain constraints on an organized research project aside from the normal ones of having to work to a fixed budget, a time schedule, employing research assistants who might be only marginally committed to the project. A variable contingency is the political and social context of the research; this creates a number of different groups to which one's work is directed; the academic community, the mass media, the official sponsor, one's own subjects. Being able to do prison research without a sponsor released us from at least one of these potentially conflicting reference groups. At the same time it increased our bond to the prisoners: there are certain trusts we cannot betray, certain information we cannot now give.

The usual sequence of encounters involved in setting up a research project was reversed in our case. The idea for the research came as much from the subjects as anyone else. We

8. An interesting discussion of work with prisoners is given by Hans Toch 'The Convict as Researcher' in Irving Horowitz and Mary Strong (eds) *Sociological Realities*, (N.Y., Harper & Row, 1971).

then took our proposals to the Assistant Governor who spoke on our behalf to the Governor who in turn commented favourably upon the research outline we submitted to the Home Office. One can see why such changes in the direction of communication are rarely adopted. For eventually the Home Office rejected our ideas for research. Fortunately we were able to reply that most of the work had already been done. We are, however, now frustrated by the Home Office's rejection of our repeated requests to visit ex-members of class who are now in other prisons and by their censorship of our letters.

The Home Office's negative attitude towards our research derives not just from concerns about security and sensationalism but rather from their suspicions that the type of methods we used were somehow not scientific. At various times we have been attacked for not using a larger sample, for not having a control group, for not using 'objective' tests, for not assessing psychological changes over a long enough period of time. We have been criticized for not assessing changes in such matters as introversion-extraversion scores, reaction times, I.Q. scores. We have already indicated our reservations about following some of these methodological injunctions; we felt further justified in our approach after evaluating a study of long-term imprisonment which was financed by the Home Office and was therefore presumably regarded by them as a model project. (A critical outline of this research is included as an appendix at the end of this volume.)

The men we met were even less impressed than we were with traditional approaches to problems of psychological change. They did not mention shifts in introversion-extraversion when we spoke to them, although they were aware of the theory and the scales used to operationalize it. Neither did they discuss decline in skills or changes in reaction time. These items did not figure on their list of effects. They were peculiarly obsessive, however, in their conversation about such mundane and untested matters as the passage of time, the making and breaking of friends, the fear of deterioration, the role of self-consciousness and the loss of identity. As we looked

39

at these matters more closely, we began to realize that the predicament of the men in E-Wing was a little less special than we had at first thought. We realized that there were many other groups of people who had faced similar psychological problems to long-term prisoners albeit in very different situations. At this point we therefore turn away from Durham prison for a while so that we can place our research into this more general context.[9]

9. Any generalizations we make from now on about long-term imprisonment are provisional in the sense that they rest on a four-year part of what odviously has to be a much longer study. Our justification for writing anything at this stage is that the first four years in the wings constituted a distinct phase in the lives of the men we know. We have every intention – given the willingness of the relevant authorities – to continue the study for its logical duration.

CHAPTER TWO

Survival in extreme situations

'Great God! This is an awful place.'

Captain Scott on life in the Antarctic

When we first talked to prisoners in E-Wing we had some
standard ideas about the problems they faced. These were
derived from our reading of the psychological literature on
sensory deprivation and the sociological studies of prison life.
But although there were elements here which were recognized
by the men, we quickly came to realize that much of this
material was not sophisticated or subtle enough to characterize
their predicament. They pointed out to us the inadequacies of
the literature, the psychologists' concern with specific sensory
rather than general psychological problems, the sociologists'
reliance upon large-scale surveys of medium-term prisoners.
Gradually we realized that we were not just trying to understand another group of prisoners. Instead we were looking at
the ways in which men in general might react to an extreme
situation, a situation which disrupted their normal lives so as
to make problematic such everyday matters as time, friendship,
privacy, identity, self-consciousness, ageing and physical deterioration. Once we realized this we were able to turn to a
range of other studies which looked at the more general
questions of how men dealt with the stress produced by any
massive disruption in their normal lives. To discuss this let
us first try to appreciate the situation when there is no such
disruption.

At such times life appears relatively orderly and meaningful
to most of us. We move from place to place with a sense of
purpose, completing one task and moving on to another; our

day is neatly divided into domestic, social and occupational routines. It is easy to forget that this smooth daily flow, this experience of the world as fairly predictable and patterned is the product of many years of learning. The infant has no such experience of regularity and continuity. Even the sensory messages it receives are jumbled and confused. The complex process we call socialization involves a resolution of this confusion. A sensory order is imposed and we are taught to assign a meaning to our social as well as our physical environment. Problems are solved and sequences – night following day, punishment following wrongdoing, rewards following hard work and good deeds – are learnt. The child decreasingly asks 'why' as the answers are dropped into place. The difficult questions, about creation, existence, death and suffering, can be postponed or expediently dealt with in terms of gods and devils.

Not that life is always so smooth. Sometimes disturbances occur in the flow but most of these are capable of resolution without profoundly affecting other parts of our life: we can pacify our wives, reassure our employers or avoid troublesome friends. Our socialization even prepares us for encountering environments, events and experiences which will raise more acute problems than these. We know adolescence will be a time of 'strain and stress', and that 'crisis points' will occur in marriage. Such familiar problems have culturally approved modes of solution ('talking it through', 'waiting for it to pass over') and specialized agencies of help and support. Disturbing events occasionally intrude from outside. Now and then we become concerned about war, religion and politics although on the whole such problems remain external.

But things are not always so familiar, problems are not always so mundane, solutions are not always available. Once in a while – and perhaps to some individuals this might never happen until they are dying – the problem is so extreme, so dreadful that one's physical existence, one's sense of self or one's whole view of the world is at risk. Sometimes the blow is sudden and physical: a motor car accident, being caught in a flood or hurricane. Sometimes it is long lasting: suffering a prolonged illness, fighting through a war, being evacuated to a strange area, or being cut off from loved ones. Such experiences have disturbing consequences: we talk of people 'going grey overnight', 'being scarred for life', 'becoming stunted' or 'crippled' or even 'never being the same again'. These experiences are literally and metaphorically shattering: they break the web of meaning we have built up around ourselves and at the same time show how fragile this web is.

Such shattering events, by disturbing the orderliness of life, may bring the meaning of life into question. People talk of 'life losing its meaning' after the death of a loved one or refer in a graphic phrase to 'the bottom falling out of their world'. But at least there is still something of that world left – 'the pieces can be picked up again' – and gradually meaning and significance return. For 'shattering' events tend to occur in one part of one's life, in one domain. This means that the other domains can then be called into service to provide reassurance, to reestablish credibility. If one has to contend with the sudden loss of a close relative, then one can keep going by 'losing oneself in one's job'. Conversely the loss of employment can be compensated for by 'retreating into the family'. Sexual failures and tensions can (if sublimation theory is correct) be translated into artistic spheres, and sorrows can be muffled by drowning them in drink.

The long-term prisoner cannot play one domain off against another in this way. When he arrives in E-Wing he has to come to terms with the fact that he is starting on a new life, one in which the routines which previously obtained in every area will be transformed. He faces up to two decades inside, two decades away from home, wife, children, job, social life and friends. He cannot reassure himself that each of these domains is merely being held in cold storage until his return – a life cannot be reassembled twenty years after its destruction. He has been given 'life' – a prison life – and somehow he must learn to live it. It is too easy to assume that prisoners are somehow ready for this experience and therefore do not suffer the same type of anxiety which would accrue to any of us were we suddenly faced with a similar predicament. It is true that a few short and medium-termers may be able to keep some things going while inside. Wives and friends can be maintained. Property can be looked after and jobs lined up ready for release, but for the long-termer the prospects in each domain are bleak. His children will not know him, his job will have disappeared, his wife may have gone and his friends will have moved away.

This type of consideration for the long-termers' situation may seem like 'bending over backwards' to do justice to his predicament, but it is only an attempt to apply the same type of sensitivity to his situation as would be brought to bear by any social scientist who was investigating the plight of the blind, the old, the infirm, the poor. Even if these prisoners are unlike such groups in that they may be thought to have 'deserved all they got', this should not influence our readiness to be sensitive about the social-psychological problems they face. Without a full consciousness of the way in which the everyday world has been broken for the long-term prisoner, we can underestimate the pains he experiences and assume that his apparent ease represents a natural adaptation to prison conditions and not one which has been personally constructed as a solution to intolerable problems.

It is this concern with being comprehensive which makes us critical of those studies which have only looked at one or two elements of an extreme situation and then attempted to generalize from them. Sensory deprivation studies provide a typical example.

Sensory and Perceptual Deprivation

Perhaps the most obvious example of the type of extreme situation we have described is to be found when radical changes occur in the physical environment. Prisoners, like explorers, space travellers and round-the-world yachtsmen clearly do have to face up to special environmental conditions of particular intensity or monotony. What sort of psychic effects do these extreme sensory and perceptual conditions have?

Studies in 'environmental psychology' (as this subfield has become known) received their first impetus from the 'coffin' experiments conducted by Donald Hebb in 1951. The environment he manufactured was not on the face of it very 'extreme', for his subjects were paid to do nothing except lie in a closed air-conditioned box and wear translucent ski goggles. The results, however, were disturbing enough. Subjects quickly asked to be released from the situation, pressing a 'panic button' to indicate their anxiety. They reported hallucinations and delusions, and claimed that they sensed their bodies in different ways. Many reported disturbing emotional symptoms. The sensory and perceptual effects obtained from this type of stimulus-deprived environment were described as being similar to mescal intoxication.

Other researchers set up similar demanding and unusual environments. One immersed his subjects in a tank of slowly flowing warm water; another placed them in a tank respirator used for poliomyelitis patients while exposing them to the blank walls of a screen or the repetitive drone of a motor. In most cases the results originally obtained by Hebb were repeated although there was a tendency for the effects to be somewhat less extreme in later studies.

There is no shortage of contemporary examples of such environmental hazards to confirm the findings of these studies. Psychologists have been widely employed in space research in attempts to counter the effects of the environmental monotony experienced by astronauts; environmental deprivation has been used in 'brainwashing' procedures and recently by the British Army in Northern Ireland in order to increase the efficiency of their interrogation procedures.

John Lilly, who has conducted a number of studies in this area, considers that the experimental work matched up well with biographical accounts of isolation and deprivation obtained from polar living and solitary sailing.

45

If one is alone long enough and at levels of physical and human stimulation low enough, the mind turns inward and projects outward its own contents and processes; the brain not only stays active despite the lowered levels of input and output, but accumulates surplus energy to extreme degrees.[1]

The result of this accumulation is an increase in fantasy but this does not appear to be satisfactory and further changes take place:

At some point a new threshold appears for more definite phenomena of regression: hallucinations, delusions, oceanic bliss etc. At this stage, given any opportunities for action or stimulation by external reality, the healthy ego seizes them and re-establishes more secondary processes. Lacking such opportunities for a long enough interval of time, reorganization takes place, how reversibly or how permanently we do not yet know.

There is a very important factor however which Lilly underestimates and other less sophisticated experimental psychologists omit from their detailed accounts, one which may accentuate or diminish the effects he describes. This is the meaning of the situation to the subjects who are involved in it.

Martin Orne, a psychologist, has pointed out that most such studies ignore this consideration. They simply expose their subject to a deprived environment and then measure his reaction. He therefore designed an experiment which he entitled 'meaning deprivation'.[2] This included all the accoutrements of the usual deprivation studies such as the screening of subjects and the presence of a 'panic' button, but the actual environment was far from 'deprived'. In fact the subjects merely had to sit in a small well-lighted room with two

1. John C. Lilly, 'Mental Effects of Reduction of Ordinary Levels of Physical Stimuli on Intact, Healthy Persons', in H. M. Proshansky, W. H. Ittelson and L. G. Rivlin (eds) *Environmental Psychology*, (London, Holt, Rinehart & Winston, 1970, pp. 221–5).

2. Martin T. Orne, 'On the Social Psychology of the Psychological Experiment' in P. G. Swingle (ed.) *Experiments in Social Psychology*, (New York, Academic Press, 1968) and M. T. Orne and K. E. Scheibe, 'The Contribution of Nonprivation Factors in the Production of Sensory Deprivation Effects: The Psychology of the "Panic Button"', *Journal of Abnormal and Social Psychology*, 68, 1964.

comfortable chairs, ice water and a sandwich. If they wanted to they could add up a list of numbers. A series of tests were given to them before and after the four-hour experiment. A control group of ten subjects received identical treatment except that they were told that they were control subjects for a sensory deprivation experiment and they had no panic button. The results showed that the experimental subjects (those with the panic button in the room) produced reactions to their situation which matched with results obtained in other studies of sensory deprivation. Without the same experience, they were nevertheless still able to show the effects. They had apparently detected the purpose of the experiment and responded in a way which they assumed was appropriate.

This experiment does not deny the effects of sensory deprivation but introduces the additional variable, meaning. If the situation is seen as 'deprived' then it is reacted to in appropriate ways. If we follow this argument, we can see that the prisoners in E-Wing are faced with a double deprivation. They are sensorily deprived (in ways we shall elaborate) and in addition they know that this is how they are meant to be. The drabness and uniformity of their concrete bunkers is intentional. In fact, any departure from these conditions is likely to produce questions in the House and allegations of mollycoddling. But most importantly, they have no panic button. They must learn to deal with sensory and perceptual deprivation for the next fifteen to twenty years. No deprivation studies have suggested the long-term psychic effects of such a sentence, but at least their inquiries into much shorter impositions have suggested the speed with which certain environments can induce psychological disturbances. If long-term prisoners do not show these effects we need to know how they combat them by restructuring the meaning of their environment.

Disaster Studies

Experimental studies of sensory deprivation are then too narrowly conceived for our purposes. Other studies of reactions

47

to extreme situations have different limitations. We looked, for example, at the material on reactions to natural disasters and massive man-made equivalents such as atomic bombardment.

These disaster studies have a great advantage over the laboratory research we have just discussed in that the situations produced by events such as floods, tornadoes, hurricanes, volcanoes are not artificial; they affect the individual's total life, not just the part which presents itself to the experimenter and they are obviously not self-imposed. One does not volunteer to be the subject of a disaster.

However, the extreme nature of the threat or the disaster itself means that the preoccupation of the population in this situation is sheer *physical* survival. The sudden nature of most disasters has led researchers to concentrate on such topics as shock, panic, mass hysteria, escape, and the perceptual distortions which lead men to miss cues of impending threats. Questions of a sociological nature have, nevertheless, been included; one classic study posed the problem of multiple group loyalties[3]: does the fireman during an explosion carry out his duties (which might help the whole community) or rush home to save his wife and family? The general problem of the recapturing of the social bonds that the disaster shatters is also a paramount concern: is there some sort of disintegration of loyalties, morals and norms, for example, through large-scale looting of shops or hoarding of rations when a flood is threatened? At least these studies deal with total other-imposed situations and not with the voluntary self-imposed conditions of the laboratory research on perceptual deprivation. In this respect they come closer to describing the 'lifer's' predicament. Unfortunately this research does not spend much time upon the social-psychological reactions to such massive disruptions.

The change in environment is so sudden and overwhelming that there is little material available about how people actually live through and experience such disasters. These studies have

3. Louis Killian, 'The Significance of Multiple Group Membership in Disaster', *American Journal of Sociology*, LVII (1952) pp. 309–14.

– for very obvious reasons – been geared to the practical question of how to minimize the destructive effects of disaster, for example, by developing early warning systems, and training communities in adaptation and survival techniques.

Surprisingly little has been written on man-made dislocations on this scale, although there is a substantial survival literature on the aftermath of the Hiroshima and Nagasaki bombings and an even greater literature on the fringes of science fiction concerned with how people might react to such events. Again it is the reactions of shock, insensibility, grief, together with the problem of social organization which receive most attention. The existence of a vast refugee problem in this century has given rise to dramatic reports about the dispossession of whole communities; here the mute faces of young children, the starved, the sick and the old are left to speak for themselves about the shattering effects of such situations.

As the novelist Nadine Gordimer writes in a foreword to a recent account of the mass displacement of Africans in South Africa: 'The physical conditions of life described in this book are such an appalling desolation that one is almost unable to think beyond bread and latrines.' But as she continues, 'Once one has got over the first shock of the physical suffering . . . one becomes increasingly aware of certain signs of another kind of suffering.' Unlike most other writers concerned with such mass phenomena she is sensitive enough to record

. . . the apathy, the peculiar listlessness of lack of hope shown by many people in the settlements, born of powerlessness to change their situation by any effort of their own, since all decisions about the circumstances of their lives are made for them.

She describes the disruption of life which we referred to earlier:

Every human life . . . has a context meshed of familiar experience – social relationships, patterns of activity in relation to environment. Call it 'home' if you like. To be transported out of this on a Government truck one morning and put down in an uninhabited place is to be asked to build not only your own shelter but your whole life over again, from scratch.[4]

It is this notion of the destruction and then the rebuilding of a life which captures the predicament of the long-termer more adequately than does the narrower focus suggested by sensory deprivation studies.

Migration

The problems created by wars, mass rehabilitation and other disasters are sometimes rather bleakly categorized as examples of involuntary migration. People are forced from their homes, they do not elect to live elsewhere. Voluntary migration has received much more extended social-psychological treatment than its involuntary variant. It has almost been a major theme in American interpretive sociology since the publication of Thomas and Znaniecki's *The Polish Peasant in Europe and America*, a study of the dislocations which had been produced by the movement of Polish migrants to America. This type of approach in migration studies has been important to us, not just because it stressed the importance and the subtlety of the individual's definition of old and new situations, but also because in the construction of such definitions, authors have recognized the need to draw upon their subjects' diaries, letters and newspapers.

It is perhaps an indication of the degree to which knowledge is compartmentalized that insights derived from migration studies have not been applied to prisoners. For these men are just as surely translated from one environment to another as any migrant. They assume different clothes, are confronted with unknown routines, new jobs, new friends, new authorities. They must change their expectations, absorb new norms, discover ways of adapting to the new situation. What Eugene Brody has to say about migration applies with only minor

4. Foreword to Cosmas Desmond, *The Discarded People*, (Penguin, 1971), p. xvii.

modifications to the prisoner entering a security wing. It is more true for this type of prisoner than any other because the régime is one to which he could not have had access before in this particular form:

Migration provides a set of concrete operations for the study of adaptation and defence in relation to social change. A shift in residence involves not only new places, but new faces and new norms. Movement over distance implies the crossing of social system boundaries, whether the systems are defined in terms of national entities, regional subcultures, or immediate friendship and kinship networks. The migrant leaves behind the support and stresses of the system from which he departs, including the push factors which contributed to his decision to move. He loses the support of social and geographic familiarity, of long-term relationships and values which were built into him while growing up. [5]

Many of these elements are relevant to the prisoner's predicament. But the critical difference between the prisoner and the migrant lies in the latter's relatively voluntary cultural and structural change. No one writes home from prison inviting those at home to join him. Prison involves an involuntary migration to a region in which the dislocations of life are not necessary costs of the move, but are rather deliberately engineered insults to the self.

Exploring and Adventure

We have also found a useful source of material in the writings of explorers and adventurers. These chronicles of weeks and months spent on the sea, in the arctic night, in the desert and the forest often contain detailed psychological descriptions of the traveller's reactions. The travellers are often literate as well as scientifically concerned about the accuracy of their observations. They have usually moved from a sophisticated civilization into an apparently bleak uncultured terrain; as they move

5. Eugene B. Brody (ed.) *Behaviour in New Environments*, (New York, Sage Publications, 1969), p. 5.

they have to deal with the cumulative physical problems of monotony and tiredness. But more interestingly they have to resolve problems about the need for their journey. Away from home, particular feats of endurance or fortitude may seem less rather than more valid. In these circumstances, whole belief systems may become insecure and the meaning of life becomes a daily concern. These men have, however, an enormous advantage over prisoners. Like the long-termers they have probably given up sensory variety, comfort, wife, friends and the satisfaction of particular reinforced routines. But this disruption of life is self-imposed for the explorer or adventurer. It is a test of strength, or faith, or courage. J. R. L. Anderson, who has considered a number of contemporary examples of personal feats in this area, observes that: 'Man knows little about himself: there is an infinite field for discovery in his own behaviour in strange physical conditions.'[6] But this does not mean that such discovery has any general value. It is almost entirely *personal*.

The world is inclined to applaud long voyages in small boats but mostly for the wrong reasons: a well-found small boat, with a crew that keeps its head, ought to be able to make a long voyage safely. It is not particularly courageous to embark on such a voyage. The challenge is in oneself – to accept discomfort, loneliness or cramped living with companions who cannot be changed, fear sometimes, short rations maybe; and to accept all these things deliberately in cold blood.[7]

The prisoner however is not rising to a challenge. He is taking his medicine. In an environment which is as bleak and apparently eternal as an arctic night, he must survive similar psychological traumas to those which preoccupy the explorer, but must survive them without being allowed any sense of achievement. If, as Maurice Herzog writes, it is 'an inconceivable experience . . . to attain one's ideal, and, at the very same

6. J. R. L. Anderson, *The Ulysses Factor*, (London, Hodder & Stoughton, 1970), p. 139.
7. ibid., p. 140.

moment to fulfil oneself',[8] then it must also be difficult to conceive of the experience of men who face similarly deprived circumstances for very long periods of time, but must face them in the knowledge that they bring no personal reward to the man who conquers them.

Studies in this area have nevertheless enabled us to see the prisoner's predicament in an unusually interesting way and have at times provided the very best accounts of some of the problems he faces. Expeditions after all do not always succeed, some even threaten loss of face rather than confirmation of self-identity. Scott's trek back from the Pole after finding the Norwegian flags is an excellent example. The environment remains challenging until the Pole is reached, even blizzards are opportunities for bravery, and chances to show one's endurance. On the journey back the sense of failure colours the landscape:

> We have been descending again, I think, but there looks to be a rise ahead; otherwise there is very little that is different from the awful monotony of past days. Great God! this is an awful place and terrible enough for us to have laboured to it without the reward of priority.[9]

Camps and Prisons

We have moved from the partial physical threats of the laboratory experiments to global physical terrors which engulf whole communities. We now turn to those distinctive extreme situations in which an individual is forcibly removed from his community and placed in a total environment from which there is no immediate escape and in which the actual date of release is uncertain (in some cases indeterminate). These environments are enforced and manipulated by others for punitive reasons. They include, of course, labour camps, concentration camps and prisons.

8. Maurice Herzog, *Annapurna*, (London, Cape, 1952), p. 193.
9. *Scott's Last Expedition. The Personal Journals of Captain R. F. Scott, C.V.O. R.N.*, (London, Murray, 1927), p. 424.

The material on concentration camps is without doubt the most intensive literature on physical and psychological survival. The testimonies of the few who came through this experience alive are virtually bench marks on which other survival attempts in our time can be measured: these were situations which were perhaps the most extreme ever devised by man against man. There are three limitations to generalizing from this literature to contemporary security prisons. The first is the obvious one that the particular combination of horrors that the camps provided have no exact replica outside their immediate cultural and historical context. The second is that the survivors have often – quite rightly – concentrated less on their own reactions, than the political nature of the system that created the camps and on trying to explain how their captors behaved in ways they did. The third – somewhat less important limitation – is that the classic accounts (such as Bettelheim's) are influenced by a particular theoretical perspective, that of psychoanalysis. This perspective is preferable to that of experimental psychology by virtue of its overriding concern with meaning, but at the same time its theoretical rigidity excludes alternative subjective interpretations.

Having said this, there is much in this literature – and accounts of allied experiences such as Russian labour camps and South African political prisons – which will directly concern us. Key themes include: (i) the extreme self-consciousness of the inmates and indeed the unambiguous recommendation of consciousness of self and others as a technique for survival; (ii) the notion that one had to resist any attempt to be changed: one had to do more than remain alive, one had to remain alive *and unchanged*; (iii) a preoccupation with having to take up an explicit position in regard to the institution: did one give in or did one fight back? and (iv) the question of whether such adverse conditions brought out the best in people or whether, on the contrary, it reduced them to an almost pre-human, animal level. We will take up these and related themes in considering the situation in a long-term security prison.

When we turn to the conventional prison literature, we are

faced with a mass of material. There are some twenty major sociological books about English, European and American prisons, countless articles and research reports as well as memoirs from the inside and literary accounts.[10]

In all such writings a picture is presented of the prison as a society in miniature, with its own culture, stratification, language and roles and its own way of accommodating to the extreme power differential between the rulers and the ruled. Some of this material is not directly relevant to us in that it is primarily of a structural kind – that is concerned with the divisions and differentiations between groups of rulers and ruled within large general prisons. Nevertheless most writers cannot resist raising questions about how the individual comes to terms with extreme situations and with how the prison subculture – the 'society of captives' – facilitates such accommodation. Descriptions tend to be couched in terms such as 'institutionalization'. This refers to a state in which the individual literally cannot survive outside the institution. While inside the walls, his behaviour is characterized by regression, apathy and listlessness. Everything has been done for him and to him and in this childlike state, he cannot make decisions any more. The spectrum here ranges from the 'institutional neurosis' described by psychiatrists to the pathetic hopelessness of the long-term petty offender who is Tony Parker's *Unknown Citizen*.[11]

Somewhat different are terms such as 'prisonization', used originally by Donald Clemmer in his classic 1940 study of an American prison.[12] This is a form of secondary socialization, in which the inmate has to learn to adapt to prison as a way of

10. A new literature has been generated in recent years in America by what has become known as 'the prison movement'. The tragic events at Attica State Prison in September 1971 (when forty-one were killed in the aftermath of an insurrection), and the life and death of George Jackson in the Californian prison system have provoked a massive interest in the prison.

11. Tony Parker, *The Unknown Citizen*, (Penguin, 1966).

12. Donald Clemmer, *The Prison Community*, (New York, Holt, Rinehart & Winston, 1958).

life. Old definitions are shattered and he has to learn how to adjust himself to the deprivations of prison. He might do this by withdrawing or, on the other hand, by continual rebellion. The range of such adjustments is dealt with in the prison literature, but in terms of a series of roles or inmate typologies, rather than through any understanding of what such adaptations mean to the individual.

These sociological approaches also try to find the link between what Gresham Sykes calls the 'pains of imprisonment' and the nature of the inmate culture.[13] Here, either by making a list of these pains, or by describing, as Goffman does, the inmate's typical career through what he calls the 'total institution' (mental hospitals, monasteries and army training camps are included as well as prisons) we obtain a detailed description of what the inmate has to contend with. Sykes, for example, lists deprivations such as those of goods and services, heterosexual relationships, security, liberty and autonomy. Goffman gives a highly sensitive account of the mortification of self the inmate has to endure as his privacy is invaded, he is programmed as a number and his old self is assaulted. These are the 'various forms of disfigurement and defilement through which the symbolic meaning of events in the inmate's immediate presence fails to corroborate his prior conception of self'.[14]

It is as an answer to these problems, according to Sykes and others, that the meaning of the inmate code can best be understood. The code represents a value system stressing loyalty, not losing one's head, not exploiting fellow inmates, not showing any weakness, asserting toughness and dignity, not being a sucker and not giving any prestige to the guards. Support – verbal at least – is given to this value system which stresses cohesion and in which the man who exemplifies the ideal ('the

13. Gresham Sykes, *Society of Captives* (Princeton, Princeton University Press, 1958). See also Gresham Sykes and Sheldon Messinger, 'The Inmate Social System' in Richard Cloward et al., *Theoretical Studies in Social Organization of the Prison*, (New, York, Social Science Research Council, 1960).

14. Erving Goffman, *Asylums*, (Penguin, 1968).

right guy') is given the highest prestige. Others' behaviour is evaluated in terms of its correspondence or divergence from this role. Goffman places somewhat less emphasis on the purely reactive elements in the system – that is, everything being a response to the pains of imprisonment – and notes how the culture is used to build up a personal reorganization in which elements of the institution actually help. That is, the culture is built around things which are *present*, rather than things *absent*.

Whatever route we take the end result is a culture which provides the inmate with a meaningful social group to identify with in his struggle. Minutely controlled, stripped of autonomy, his self image under severe attack, the inmate solves some of his problems through absorption of the inmate code. As the inmates move towards greater solidarity so – it is suggested – the pains of imprisonment become less severe and – in the recent politicized version of this theme – they come to understand their true nature as a 'convict class'.

And in Another Prison

Without going into this literature in any depth at this stage, it is clear that it comes close to the phenomenological problems of survival in extreme situations which we raised at the beginning of this chapter. Close, but not close enough. The delineation of the inmates' problems and how the subculture partially solves them will for the most part be taken for granted by us. What we would like to stress is the conscious, creative nature of the subculture rather than seeing it simply as a set of prescriptions or a network of roles. Literary accounts tend to give more credibility to such creative elements than do sociological analyses, and for the same reason (although we are sceptical about such notions as the 'convict class' and even more so about seeing prisoners as the vanguard of the revolution) we find the prison movement's emphasis on the conscious and creative nature of the prisoner's struggle relevant to our own interests.

Our argument throughout this book is that the culture does

not merely operate in a negative way, as a system of social control: this plays down the positive nature of the dogmas, mythologies, beliefs, modes of adaption and feeling which are part of day to day experience of people who find themselves in extreme situations. It is these banal, everyday, taken-for-granted issues we are concerned with, plus at a loftier extreme what Berger and Luckmann called the person's 'symbolic universe'. Socialization involves giving the individual conceptual machineries to maintain his universe. He has to develop a picture which is not just orderly but which is plausible and explains or justifies his experience. Such legitimation 'not only tells the individual why he should perform one action and not another; it also tells him why things are as they are'.[15]

What we are interested in is how, under extreme situations, people cope with universes changing, machineries being sabotaged and pictures being blurred or wholly obliterated. This then, is not another book about a prison. It is an account of how one small group of men, long-term security risk prisoners in one type of English prison during the 1960s, dealt with their environment. We feel justified in calling this environment extreme because of its physical characteristics (the cells, locks, confined space), its sensory deprivations (sound, colour, variety), its restrictions on social and sexual intercourse and its special psychological character as an authoritarian, punitive and relatively permanent régime. We are not directly interested in the total social systems – made up both of criminals and social control agencies – in which the group can be located, nor do we look in detail at the inmate codes, roles, and patterns of leadership. We have little to say about the modification of criminal values that ties up with therapeutic treatment, or rehabilitative interests. It would be simplest to say that we have been – and continue to be – engaged on a longitudinal study of the psychological reactions of a small group of men to an extreme and immutable environment, imposed upon them as a punishment.

15. Peter Berger and Thomas Luckmann, *The Social Construction of Reality*, (London, Allen Lane The Penguin Press, 1971).

Starting with the group members' perception of this environment we have tried to construct, with their help, a phenomenology of the security wing: how life there is given meaning, how one passes time, how friends are made and lost, how one resigns oneself to the environment and how one resists it. We have, in other words, looked at quite commonplace matters such as time, work, friendship and self identity but looked at them in a world in which so much of the taken-for-granted elements in everyday life are problematic and even disturbing.

Once we have depicted this day-to-day prison world, we attempt in the last chapters to relate it to such complex 'external' matters as the personal biographies of the prisoners, and the ideologies to which they may subscribe and to which they may turn for reassurance in their predicament.

CHAPTER THREE

The closed emotional world of the security wing

'It's like living in a submarine.'
Paul, one of the prisoners, on life in the wing

The atmosphere in Durham maximum security wing differs from that in other parts of the prison. There are no long lines of prisoners moving in and out of the building, no sudden bursts of sound, no crowded rooms, no clanking machinery. This building is designed for no other purpose than successfully to contain its inmates. Its success is measured exclusively by its impregnability.

After going through the three sets of gates which admit you to the main prison, it takes approximately ten minutes to get into the wing. You are led between the dogs by an officer, then scrutinized through a peep-hole before the first double-locked door of the actual wing is opened from the inside. This admits you to an antechamber in which you wait until more routine signals are exchanged by officers on both sides of another double-locking door. Once through this, you find yourself standing on the specially thickened concrete ground floor of the block. Above tower the familiar metal cat-walks. Your walk along the ground floor arcade to the metal stairs which lead to the first landing is further scrutinized from a spy-hole in a door at the far end of the block; each corner on the way up to the meeting room on the second floor is controlled by an officer.

After all these elaborate precautions, it comes as a surprise to find the building so empty. There are no prisoners to be seen. Although there are nearly sixty cells in the wing, only a few are occupied. It is rather like the lions' cage at Whipsnade: after all the wire and spikes and notices, it is slightly absurd to find that the objects of all this attention are not readily visible. The analogy is not one that escapes the prisoners. During the 1968 riot when the prisoners seized their own records and read the reports which had been written about them, one found that a chaplain had referred to him as an animal. On his next pastoral visit to the man's cell he was greeted by a savage roar.

In fact the four floors of the security wing we studied rarely housed more than twenty prisoners at any one time. There were nevertheless always plenty of prison officers to be seen, peering through glass windows in doors, sitting in their office cells, leaning over the landing rails and exchanging words with their mates on other levels through the anti-suicide netting. The officers always outnumbered the prisoners by about two-to-one, a staffing requirement which meant that officers were regularly called upon to remain inside the wing after their normal working day, or night, was over. Shifts of up to fifteen hours were not unusual. It was overtime which their economic situation hardly allowed them to refuse.

The relative emptiness of the place, the open landings, the high ceiling above the 'fours', were not enough to relieve the sense of claustrophobia experienced by staff, prisoners and visitors to the wing. It was not just the presence of so many locks and keys which created this feeling – these are after all a standard element in all prisoners' and prison officers' lives and had become a familiar aspect of life inside for many of the recidivists in E-Wing – but rather the completely lifeless atmosphere of the entire building. This was the claustrophobia of the tomb, rather than the crowded lift. The lighting was completely uniform, there were no shadows or pools of light (although at least at Durham the neon uniformity was not too intense – in another security wing, where closed circuit television is constantly used, the lighting has to be permanently maintained at a higher level of brightness). There were no colour variations in the wing at all, no distinctive clothes, merely two sets of uniforms (a move to allow lifers to wear some of their own clothes brought questions in the House and a swift indication from the Home Office that such liberalization was not intended).

There were no windows which opened in this building to let in any air, so the great concrete and steel vault throbbed day and night, winter and summer, to the rhythm of an inadequate ventilation system. The outside world was totally excluded. Even the suggestion that an additional fan might be installed to cool one particularly oppressive room was rejected for a long time on the grounds that even the smallest air chink in the wall would allow external enemies to introduce poisoned gas into the wing. This was then a lifeless cavern of railings and landings and pipes. 'It's like living in a submarine,' as Paul said. And, of course, for these prisoners the voyage was measured in decades, not months.

Long-term prisoners did not spend their entire time in the wing. An exercise yard had been attached to the building, a small round, high-fenced compound. At the top of the wire fence, the barbed wire curved inward and down to make escape by climbing impossible. We were told that professional soldiers had been used to test the security precautions here. Their failure to escape had meant that the prisoners were allowed to walk through a low concrete corridor from E-Wing and emerge rather like Roman gladiators into the barbed wire arena outside.

The environment at Durham was by no means unique. The special security wing at Leicester is regarded as even more claustrophobic by inmates. It consists of one floor, approximately twenty-five yards long and five yards wide. At times there have been fourteen officers and two T.V. cameras to watch over seven inmates.

Particular social and physical environments, however extreme, do not have automatic consequences for the social-psychological life of their inhabitants (as we have argued earlier in relation to the sensory deprivation studies). One may rather talk of them placing certain general limits upon patterns of daily life. They raise questions about matters which are taken for granted in other contexts. In this chapter we particularly consider the problems of sociability and privacy, the problems of friendship and loneliness in the type of environment we have described.

Relationships Inside

When we are in trouble, when we experience anxiety or disturbance in our normal life, we look around for other people who are similarly placed in order that we can modify the distressing effects by collectively constructing reassuring accounts. The presence of an intimate also opens up the possibility of a distraction, of a reduction in the saliency of the distressing circumstances. It has even been shown by social psychologists that anxious people derive some comfort from the mere physical proximity of others, even if communication is prohibited. In the maximum security wing therefore, the circumstances which normally impel one to seek an intimate or friend are heightened. But the usually taken-for-granted nature of friendship is surrounded with problems in this environment.

In the first place there is the difficulty of actually finding a companion. There are usually only twenty other prisoners to choose from and there are certain restrictions upon choice even within this limited number. These men have nearly all been imprisoned for extreme acts of deviance, and the prospect of association with some of them may induce as much anxiety as does the prospect of facing life in the security wing alone. These prisoners, like most people, have a fear of being contaminated by certain sorts of deviance, a fear of being personally affected through contact with other individuals. As the American sociologist, Gresham Sykes, remarks in his discussion of a much larger security prison:

> While it is true that every prisoner does not live in the constant fear of being robbed or beaten, the constant companionship of thieves, rapists, murderers and aggressive homosexuals is far from reassuring.[1]

1. Gresham Sykes, *The Society of Captives:* A Study of a Maximum Security Prison, (Princeton, Princeton University Press, 1958), p. 77.

63

Even this qualified comment is an overstatement in relation to the situation we studied. The prisoners we met were worried about contamination but only by one other type of inmate – the sex offender. The criminal careers of the other men, robbery, protection, murder, were not divisive factors, they did not provide a basis for either friendship or enmity. This is not to say that these men are not aware of each other's distinctive derelictions or that old gang loyalties or personal feuds are forgotten, but only that there is a self-conscious decision to play down such matters in the interest of group solidarity.

But all these men distinguish themselves sharply from sex offenders. The distinction is physically marked in the wing by the segregation of the sex offenders on a separate landing. This top landing can only be reached by negotiating another locked gate. We spent some time on this top floor although our regular class initially disapproved of such visits. The 'ordinary' prisoners had little contact with the men on the 'fours' although there were opportunities for them to meet each other. We were completely unsuccessful in our attempts to invite men from the top floor down to our classes on the lower. The 'lower' class objected declaring that the others were 'monsters' or 'animals', although they recognized the hypocrisy or at least the irony involved in the application of such crude labels. As David said: 'We know it's a prejudice, but we just have to differentiate ourselves from them.' Gradually, however, we became aware that this was not an absolute differentiation. Some softening of the rejection takes place over time. Some sex offenders are eventually admitted to limited interaction, although not chosen as intimates, whilst others are still rigidly excluded. A sexual offender, whose 'madness' is regarded as passive, for example, and who displays a certain pathetic quality is more easily tolerated than an offender who has committed a similar crime but who exhibits a certain sense of self-consciousness about what he has done or displays an ideological arrogance about his pre-prison deviant life style.

If the offender's behaviour can be seen as a variation on a recognizable perversion then he may also have his humanity partially restored. Buggery, bestiality and rape can all be encompassed. But Paul's attempt on one occasion to justify a particularly aberrant piece of sexual behaviour on the grounds of its similarity to normal sexual practice, broke down when he tried to allow the deviant a degree of self-consciousness about his 'perverted' behaviour. It could only be acceptable as long as the individual 'did not know what he was doing'. (Not that this preference for particular motivational accounts is confined to long-term prisoners. Its existence amongst middle-class magistrates has been described by one of us in a piece of research which was very much influenced by group discussions on the normality of 'sexual deviance' in the wing.)[2]

This anxiety about close relationships with sex offenders means that there are a reduced number of prisoners from whom to select a companion. The average short-term prisoner can find friends from amongst his cell-mates, or from the hundreds of men in his block; he may select a companion from his work-place, or from the library. In the security wing there is no alternative but to choose from the small group of notorious prisoners who share every minute of his daily life. The short-term prisoner may even manage without close friends, having little anxiety about the length of his sentence to dissipate and enjoying regular visits from a family or wife to whom he will return within a few years.

Standard texts on prison life are often reassuring about social relationships within the prison, not just because they are typically describing larger prisons where there is more choice available, but also because of their assumptions about the possibilities of interaction between staff and inmates. Sykes observes that: 'Guards and prisoners are drawn from the same culture and they hold many of the same values and beliefs. They share a common language and a common historical experience.'

In their pioneering study of a large English maximum security

2. Laurie Taylor, 'The Significance and Interpretation of Motivational Accounts: The Case of Sex Offenders', *Sociology*, (January 1972).

prison, Pentonville, Terence and Pauline Morris illustrate in detail the common predicaments of the staff and prisoners and their cultural affinities. In terms of social aspirations and achievements, they are heir to a common culture, the urbanized working class.

Their speech is punctuated by the same idioms, they employ the same swear words, they both carry little tins of tobacco and cigarette papers. In behaviour and attitudes they also exhibit marked cultural affinity; they have strong views about women going to work, about sex and about the colour question; they read the same newspapers and have similar tastes in entertainment ... It was striking how in the matter of eating habits, some officers were indistinguishable from prisoners.[3]

In E-Wing very few of these similarities applied. The prisoners might have had the same socio-economic origins as the prison officers, but they shared very little in later experience and contemporary culture or language. They go out of their way to differentiate themselves from the officers on the landing. It would not be going too far to say that they felt in some danger of being contaminated by what they regard as the dull, prejudiced, lumpen-proletarian nature of their guards. Their jokes were often at the officers' expense. When David was asked by an officer about what he had learnt in class that night, he explained carefully that they had been discussing a report which showed that prison officers were predominantly 'authoritarian psychopaths'. The officer's cheery satisfaction with the reply was a source of amusement amongst many of the men for several weeks. It was not that the prisoners simply felt intellectually superior, but also that they felt culturally distinct. They were predominantly from London, they had a metropolitan smartness which they contrasted with the dull peasant mentality of their provincial guardians. The only sign of feeling for the officers had a patronizing quality. The most sympathetic and at the same time the most revealing comment came from Roy, one of the better-known members of the wing. He

3. Terence and Pauline Morris, *Pentonville: A Sociological Study of An English Prison*, (London, Routledge & Kegan Paul, 1963), p. 99.

observed that 'screws not only had to spend as many waking hours in the wing as the inmates, but also that when they got home at night and got into bed, their wives turned to them and said: "Darling, did you speak to Roy today?"'

This awareness of their public image also set them apart from the officers. They all know the truth about famous murders and robberies, whilst their guards, despite their proximity to the agents of such enterprises, have to rely upon mass media interpretations. Prisoners in the security wings have a strong sense of personal status; they are still frequently referred to in newspapers and on television, and they rigorously dissociate themselves from petty criminals – the 'gas meter bandits' – of the rest of the prison. This sense of status is quite strong enough to exclude the screw from being chosen for social relationships. The Governor or the Assistant Governor are more likely to be viewed as potential colleagues. At least they are accorded intelligence and their motives are presumed to be honourable. They are not, like the screws, doing the job because there is nothing else they could do. But long-term relationships with Governors are just as impossible as those with fellow prisoners. Promotion and transfer of administrative staff break down relationships as insensitively and suddenly as do routine arbitrary movements of men from wing to wing.

Relationships Outside: Letters and Visits

It is not just inside contacts which are a problem; the long-termer is also gradually losing his outside contacts. Old gang loyalties quickly disappear once the leader or lieutenant has been inside a few years and there is a growing problem involved in retaining contact with wives and children. You suddenly realize as Roy said that 'you want *their* letters more than they want *yours*'. There are occasional passages in outsiders' letters which suggest that they have not read the prisoners' letters too carefully, or that other events have forced the contents out of their minds. Either way, a sense of the unilateralism of the relationship grows upon the lifer. A concern about how long it will last

67

begins to undermine the reassurances which accompanied the initial separation.

This concern is undoubtedly realistic. It is just not possible for many prisoners to believe that wives or friends will wait for twenty years. There is already enough anxiety in the prospect of half a life in prison without the additional worry which is involved in anticipating a 'Dear John' letter. There may almost be some fatalistic relief in reducing the emotional reliance upon outsiders. It increases the individual's autonomy; it ensures that the absence of visitors or letters is not a recurrent worry, and that such absences do not provide opportunities for patronizing sympathy by officers.

The whole subject of letter writing can easily become one which involves the prisoner in endless frustration. A form of censorship operates which in effect prevents the prisoner from writing about the one subject that matters most to him: his own situation. As two ex-prisoners noted simply: 'There is plenty that happens in prison to write about – the problem is that one is not permitted to write about what actually happens.'[4] Then there are also restrictions on the number of letters which may be written (the maximum is two a week, one of which has to be purchased out of the prisoners' money), and upon the people to whom they may be sent. One may, for example, not initiate any correspondence with private individuals not known before entering prison, one may not write to any M.P. other than one's own and letters to organizations such as the National Council for Civil Liberties, Radical Alternatives to Prison, Release and even the International Commission on Human Rights may be suppressed by the Home Office after referral by the Governor. There are a number of reasons which will lead a prisoner's letter to be referred to 'P 3' (the section of the Home Office which deals with the censorship of correspondence). In some cases Governors have standing instructions to refer all the letters written by certain prisoners to P 3 before posting them. The list of reasons for internal censorship is

4. Howard Levy and David Miller, *Going to Jail: The Political Prisoner*, (New York, Grove Press, 1971), p. 42.

almost unlimited. The following is a random selection from those provided at one prison (not Durham) over a six month period:

OUTGOING LETTERS

Reason for referral to Governor (by censor)	Governor's Comments and Decision
'Sir, can something be done about this type of letter, i.e. Remarks made on cartoon cutting.'	Rewrite
'He mentions he has had two letters stopped.'	Stop and Rewrite
'A disturbed letter.'	Rewrite
'Complaints and moans.'	Rewrite
'Complaints about hostel management "pigs".'	Rewrite
'To *News of World*.'	Stop
'Complains of treatment.'	Stop and Rewrite
'Letter to second M.P.'	Stop
'Complains about lack of medical treatment.'	Stop
'Page 2 of letter to brother in Borstal. Talk of C.I.D. pig.'	Stop and Rewrite
'Page 3 – not too keen on the censor.'	Stop
'Written in red ink. Thought inmates were not allowed red ink pens.'	Rewrite
'Complains about no tea for visitors. "We are inhuman."'	Stop
'Attempting to get pen friend.'	Stop
'Is this man in his right mind. Tells his solicitor about the drains.'	No. Please post
'Applying for 2 books on occult. Not knowing this inmate, I wonder about their suitability for him.'	Please post
'Top of 2nd page. "Three quarters of the staff are idiots".'	Rewrite
'A disgusting outgoing letter.'	Stop. Rewrite. Grossly improper language

If sending letters out is a difficult business, exposing oneself as it does to the absurdities of the censorship system, then it is no easier to receive letters. Incoming letters are all seen by the censor; he immediately weeds out all those from people who are not on the prisoner's official list of correspondents. No letters from sympathizers are allowed through. This accounts for the bulk of the suppressions but in addition letters from friends will be withheld if they make any reference to prison conditions or discuss the prisoner's predicament in any but the most abstract terms.

Whilst censorship of outgoing letters may be frustrating, suppression of incoming letters has an even worse effect upon those attempting to keep links with outside society. Once a letter from a friend outside is suppressed, the prisoner has no way of knowing that it was even sent. He is merely left to presume that he has been deserted by others. The friend on the outside cannot inform him otherwise. If he tells another correspondent to pass on news of his attempts to write, then this letter will in its turn be suppressed. In these ways contact with outside can break down completely after a man with a life sentence has served only a couple of months of his time.

What the Category A prisoners lack in the way of correspondence with the outside world cannot be made up for by visits. Officially, visits may only be made by wives and blood relations and are limited to periods of thirty minutes every eight weeks. However, Governors and the Home Office can show some flexibility in the enforcement of these regulations. Visits by 'approved' friends with no criminal records may be allowed and the frequency of visits may be increased, so that, in some cases, a visit every fortnight is granted. Nevertheless the restrictions upon the length of visits and upon who may visit are still harsh. Wives who have to travel several hundred miles every fortnight if they are to keep any contact with their husbands are hardly satisfied with the thirty-minute conversation to which they may be limited when they arrive.

All visitors are extensively vetted. Their special status is underlined by the fact that they have to submit a photograph of

70

themselves to prevent impersonation occurring. Any person may be excluded from visiting for no stated reason. One member of our class – Ray – was denied a visit from his wife for nearly a year because she had a criminal record. (Her crime consisted of harbouring Ray after he had committed an offence of which she declared herself to have no knowledge.) The prisoners particularly resent the way in which departures from the rules can be presented by governors as examples of official liberality. Their only means of contacting the outside world become a matter of negotiation with the authorities and therefore dependent upon good behaviour.[5] Even when visits do take place, they are inevitably closely monitored by Prison Officers and personal contact is minimized (for example, children are not allowed to sit on their father's lap). The conduct of the prisoner during the visit is considered an important indicator of his progress and is noted in the daily diary which is kept on every Category A man.

We have itemized only a few of the frustrating elements in the area of visiting and correspondence. Most prisoners could describe many more. Such matters become a constant source of anxiety and concern. In these circumstances it is not surprising that contacts with outside breakdown or are consciously reduced by the prisoners. There is some pattern in the way in which this breakdown occurs.

Nearly thirty years ago Maurice Farber produced a highly sensitive account of life in an American prison, which describes the problems of outside relationships in terms of the amount of suffering that the presence of such relationships produces. His long and intimate interviews with prisoners revealed that the relationship between suffering and contact with the outside was curvilinear. Those who had few contacts with the outside through letters and visits were low in suffering, those who had medium contact suffered a great deal, while those who had

5. It is significant that the recently formed prisoners' union, P.R.O.P. (Preservation of the Rights of Prisoners), considers it of central importance to transform the 'privileges' relating to visits and letters into *rights*.

high contact were again found to be low in suffering. Farber's interviews were with long and short-term prisoners, so generalization is difficult. But he found clear evidence of prisoners who cut off all contact in order to reduce suffering. As one said: 'I don't do hard time. It's much easier if you get the outside off your mind and just forget about your family, your folks and your wife.'[6]

The curvilinear relationship suggests that prisoners take an 'all or nothing-at-all attitude'. Either one attempts to keep everything going, to continue to live vicariously with wife and children and friends, or one abandons oneself to the prison community. The middle state in which relationships are only tenuously maintained seems least bearable. It is difficult to see how, over very long periods, high outside contact can be consistently maintained given the restrictions on writing and visiting which we have described. We predict that those few – and they are very few – who maintain high outside contact at the moment will have to suffer considerably over the years until their links become so tenuous that they are led towards the more popular and less worrying position of low contact. Of course there are those who do not have to face this dilemma. An American prisoner writes:

One of the reasons I always did easy time was I had nobody who would write or visit me. Also, I had no life outside. My mind was usually always in the here and now. I lived a day at a time and had no thoughts of the streets or getting out. Most of the dudes I knew had a family or friends who would write to them and sometimes they got a visit. Every night if they didn't get a letter, they would pace the floor worrying about why their people didn't write. It was the same way with visits. If they didn't get an expected visit they would bug out.[7]

6. Maurice Farber, 'Suffering and Time Perspective of the Prisoner', Part IV of Kurt Lewin (ed.) *Studies in Authority and Frustration*, (University of Iowa, *Studies in Child Welfare*, vol. XX, 1944), p. 176.

7. 'One Who's There', *County Time*, (San Francisco, Connections, p. 10).

Some indication of the way relationships break down is provided by data obtained from our Eccleston sample. We asked eighteen Category A prisoners who had served approximately one third of their sentence about visits and letters. Half the men had not been visited in the last month, and of these four had not been visited for three years. For the majority, of the men, visits were now less regular and their attempts to make new contacts in the outside world had either failed or been suppressed. Only half the men received letters as frequently as when they arrived and most of them said they felt more isolated. There was some evidence here that men had deliberately severed all contacts early in their sentence.[8]

There is another factor which influences the cutting down on outside contacts. This is the awareness of personality changes which tend to make previous outside relationships less viable. These prisoners have not only developed themselves physically while they have been in jail, they have also developed mentally. They are engaged in educational courses of varying complexity; if permission were granted there are several who would have little difficulty in obtaining degrees from correspondence courses or from the Open University. Many of the men we know write extensively. Jock recently produced a 20,000-word paper for us on his life in the army, David regularly writes a thousand words of a novel every day, while Alec turns out short essays about his childhood. The amount of reading done by these prisoners is also impressive. Three or four books are read in a week, the complete works of Freud or Dickens may be read at a stretch. David wrote to tell us that: 'Louis is at the moment reading the works of William Shakespeare (the complete works by the sound of it) and we exchange terribly literary letters about the sonnets with which I'm familiar.'

8. Further confirmation – of a somewhat different order – of this pattern can be found in Timothy Leary's semi-mystical Joycean ramblings about his prison experience: 'Letters very important to prisoner who has outside love tie. But outside love ties are impossible and sensible inmate immediately detaches from his ex-mate (Go wild crazy berserk).' Timothy Leary, *Jail Notes*, (New York, Douglas Books, 1970), p. 60.

Such intellectual work undoubtedly allows the men a chance to realize certain goals in an otherwise relatively undifferentiated future but it also offers them a chance of finding some sophisticated articulations of their predicament. The work is far from being a mere endurance exercise – a shallow ritual. The men refer to the dramatic changes that this or that book has produced in their view of life. They talk of their personality as changing as a result of what they have read, and they recognize the cumulative nature of these changes.

Not all long-term prisoners share these literary concerns but such intellectual involvement provides another reason for the gradual moving away from reliance upon outsiders as friends. Relatives do not know how it is inside in quite the same way that Serge or Solzhenitsyn know. The importance of their sympathy may be gradually undermined by their failure to keep pace with changes in the prisoner's perception of his environment and of himself. Visiting hours are too short, the length of letters too restricted, to allow any adequate communication of these matters to outsiders. This is important for we do not mean to say that prisoners independently or naturally in the course of time move away from outside contacts.

Perhaps the significance of visiting is not apparent to those who are well away from the actual situation in the wings. 'A visit' sounds a casual matter – it sounds dispensable in the interests of security if one defines it in orthodox social terms. But these are not just brief intrusions from the outside world; when this link breaks the individual must rely completely upon the inmate culture or upon his own resources. There are no other directions available.

To summarize: in a situation where friends are particularly needed there are special difficulties placed in the way of making or maintaining them. The small number of inmates, the presence in this number of certain undesirables and the alien character of the prison officers, combine to make inside choice of companions difficult, while at the same time links with outside intimates become tenuous because of difficulties over visits and letters, changes in the personality and sensibility of the inmates, and because of the impossible prospect of twenty years' physical separation.

The Dilemma of Friendship

All these restrictions upon choice of contacts mean that one remains friendless or that typically just one other person is selected as a companion. There is also a good social-psychological reason why close dyadic relationships develop. For these men, who are forced to restrict their friends by the circumstances of the wing would, in any case, have difficulty in maintaining a network of friends in the way in which we normally do outside.

In everyday life we typically have several friends, several other people whom we rely upon for reassurance about our intellectual, ethical or sexual attributes. We may go to our wife or girl-friend for reassurance about our sexual ability, we will make use of another friend for career advice, and perhaps another for intellectual reassurance. The fact that we have several friends whom we use on different occasions and before whom we can strike different poses does not make any of them dispensable. Indeed, there is a considerable anguish felt at losing 'someone with whom we can really talk', or 'someone with whom we can have a good night out', even though we may not regularly avail ourselves of these opportunities for talking or carousing.

In the security wing one cannot have someone to talk to at work, someone to laugh with at leisure, for the audience is always the same and the choice of companions the same. There is one set of characters and one stage – the typical shifting from place to place and group to group which is common in outside life and even in larger prison populations is not possible. There is little role segregation, little opportunity for the presentation of different selves in different contexts. In such circumstances, a single personal relationship may be called upon to sustain the various functions which would be spread across several other friends in outside life. One's friend in the security wing is not simply there for sex, or intellectual chats, or discussion of personal anxieties, or humour, or solidarity against alien forces – but for *all* these things. Inevitably the relationship is very close. But such intense relationships are not likely to last very long. Home Office policy in relation to the maximum security wings involves moving inmates from one wing to another without warning. To quote from a recent letter: 'As you may have seen from the press Louis has left us. I am a "bit sick" because he was a close friend. In these places, you get to know people really well and Louis was one of the best . . .'

When a man loses his friend in these conditions, there is no point in trying to maintain the relationship. Letters between the divided men are unlikely to be allowed, and if one gets out of prison before the other, he cannot visit his friend because of his criminal record. Under these circumstances, friends have to be quickly dropped following a move and new alliances sought. As the letter went on to say:'Louis was my close friend and constant companion for over a year yet now he has gone to Parkhurst and I accept, almost without thinking, that I will not see him again.'

The intensity of relationships between men, an intensity which is often reinforced by sexual concerns in these deprived circumstances, and the suddenness of the break which occurs in the relationship make for a highly charged emotional atmosphere in the wings. 'The place is like a girls' school,' complained one of the men. This is certainly an incestuous setting; the men wish they could go to a bigger prison and object to the present dispersal system on the grounds that it forces them to live in highly charged emotional enclaves.

The following extract from an interview describes the situation.

Martin. At least in a bigger prison, it's closer to normal. If you get angry with someone, or he gets on your nerves, you can always get away from him for a while; go to another wing or another landing till it blows over. But here it's impossible, there's no escape, you can't get more than twenty feet away from anyone.

Stan. So you think that most people in these wings would like to move to bigger places?

Martin. Yes, even though that might mean giving up some of the physical facilities we have here.

Not that these problems will necessarily be resolved when the men move to larger wings. We asked the men in Eccleston to describe the difficulties which they found in making friends in prison. These men – in this case our sample was made up of forty-two long-termers – did not of course have many of the restrictions upon making friends which were present in E-Wing. They were nevertheless in relatively confined security conditions and obviously found that the making of friends in these circumstances was a very real problem.

Nearly one half of the group described the chief difficulty about friendship in prison in terms of the deep involvement it entailed. They talked about getting 'too close for safety' and referred to the way in which one could easily get hurt by completely confiding in one other person. Complete involvement with one other person was said to be dangerous because of the hurt which could then be produced by his being moved away ('you wake up and they are gone') or by his decision to adopt another prisoner as a companion. A majority of the prisoners said that they quite deliberately avoided the complexities which could result from such a close relationship, although at the same time they admitted the especially great need for friends which prison induced.

One Eccleston prisoner described the interpersonal situation in the following way:

One is subject to intense pressures by virtue of one's imprisonment and one tends to regress to childhood, to the stage where little things mean a great deal. As our feelings are linked directly to external influences over which we have no control, people tend to be hypersensitive, and as with children take it out on those closest to them, i.e. their close friends, i.e. a letter arrives late or doesn't arrive and this is enough to cause murder.

Although Eccleston is larger than E-Wing, it is clearly not big enough to eliminate the possibilities of highly charged interpersonal relationships. The comments made by the prisoners on the questionnaire echoed the more extended statements we collected in Durham.

The strains induced on friendship by physical proximity in a confined space are sensitively portrayed by Richard Byrd, writing specifically about two-man relationships under such conditions as an isolated camp:

... once the simple tasks of the day are finished, there is nothing else to do but take each other's measure. Not deliberately. Not maliciously. But the time comes when one has nothing left to reveal to the other; when even his unformed thought can be anticipated, his pet ideas become a meaningless drool, and the way he blows out his pressure lamp or drops his boots on the floor or eats his food become a rasping annoyance ... In a polar camp, little things like that have the power to drive even disciplined men to the edge of insanity ... There is no escape anywhere. You are hemmed in on every side by your own inadequacies and the crowding pressures of your associates.[9]

Privacy

The continual surveillance by another (which Byrd talks about) should attune us to another problem which exists alongside the special nature of friendships in the wing. It is not just that friends are limited, that they have to be selected from inside, that they will tend to serve several functions, and that they will be suddenly lost for ever – this is only one aspect of the abnormal social situation of the long-term prisoner. In addition to this perversion of normal social relationships, he is faced with a complete lack of privacy.

Again, as in the case of friendship, this word needs to be taken apart in order that the assumptions involved in its everyday use can be made clear. Superficially we may not be particularly impressed when we hear that prisoners lack privacy; it sounds very much like a condition that those outside

9. Richard Byrd, *Alone*, (London, Putnam, 1938), pp. 16–17.

prison frequently experience and which has no serious psychological implications.

But when we look at the concept of privacy carefully we can start to make distinctions which have serious implications for long-term prisoners. Following an analysis made by the American political scientist A. F. Westin, we can distinguish four basic states of privacy: solitude, intimacy, anonymity and reserve.[10] Solitude refers to the state in which the person is alone and unobserved by others – a state of complete isolation. This never obtains in the maximum security wing. There are 'Judas holes' in every cell door and in one wing electronic devices under the floor enable prison officers to monitor the actual movements of the prisoners in their cells.

In addition there may be closed circuit television cameras which necessitate the use of strong light in all areas of the wing and from whose eyes not even the prison officers can escape. We have been given examples of officers who justify the enforcement of petty restrictions by reference to the camera. 'Don't blame me. It's the camera's fault.' One prisoner described the paranoia induced by such continuous observation in the following way.

This tomb, this electronic torture chamber bound with eyes ... camera eyes ... and the dead unfeeling eyes of the state's cossacks.

And another wrote to describe his wing:

It is very claustrophobic here, very small wing, if you can imagine a world of twenty-five yards long by five yards wide. This is where we spend most of the day except for two one-hour exercise periods in the yard. You would never believe the microscopic surveillance that takes place here with television camera eyes and the eyes of warders. It literally is a dehumanizing chamber.

Solitude is typically required in everyday life that we can go out of play for a while. Complete isolation from observation,

10. A. F. Westin, *Privacy and Freedom*, (London, Bodley Head, 1970).

and from sudden intrusion are necessary conditions for indulgence in private fantasies, for obtaining a sense of individuality. Attempts to find solitude – and the related states of privacy – are a central feature of what Goffman in *Asylums* calls 'the underlife of a total institution'. He describes in detail how inmates try to obtain protection from official surveillance through going to *free places* (places shared with any other inmate) and *group territories* (places shared with a few selected inmates). Here, in corners of the hospital garden or out-of-the-way work places, the inmates withdraw temporarily from authority. Such withdrawal is rarely possible in E-Wing. Though the prisoners have some private territory in the form of their own cells the structure and size of the building, together with the security measures, hardly allow for any free places.

But if there is no opportunity for solitude, there is even less for the second state of privacy – intimacy. This refers to the type of privacy sought by two or even more people who wish to achieve maximum personal affinity. This again sounds a minor matter until we reflect upon the energy that most of us put into its achievement. Typically it involves not merely freedom from the presence of others but also the exclusion of distracting noises and sounds, an exclusion which we often effect in domestic and social situations by the use of gentle lighting, soft music and the removal of the telephone from its hook. We might think of this sort of privacy as expendable until we imagine a life in which the opportunity for the construction of such an intimate environment never existed.

The third state of privacy, which Westin describes as anonymity, refers to the seeking and achieving of freedom from identification and observation in public places. It is the presence of such anonymity which allows one to relax in different settings. One can switch off, drop out and not be a subject of comment for so doing. This type of anonymity is often available for offenders in large prisons. But in the maximum security wing everyone is known to everyone else. In such circumstances anonymity for even a few moments is impossible.

This predicament is shared with physically stigmatized persons, who are continual objects of public attention.[11] The prisoners have a dual lack of anonymity: not only are they open to being approached and addressed by anyone in the wing, but their identities are public knowledge and therefore anything they do or say can be transformed into a story.

The remaining private state of reserve is defined by a person's ability not to reveal certain aspects of himself that are particularly personal or shameful. The security wing is not conducive to reserve. Every prison officer knows in detail the lives of the men he observes. Their mail is read, their visitors' conversations overheard, their life histories are available on record for general inspection. Their health problems are matters for public discussion. They are watched during the performance of intimate toilet functions. Their domestic problems become public troubles. As Jock said:

. . . being locked up with small groups of six to ten can be unbearable at times. One of our number only has to have trouble with family or be out of sorts and everybody suffers with him – where one could get away from this kind of poisonous atmosphere in a larger unit.

It may seem long-winded to draw out all these aspects of privacy, but it is important to stress that whilst we may intermittently endure the absence of one or other states – we may for example regret the lack of solitude on our holiday, the absence of intimacy in our office, the impossibility of anonymity in the town's only night spot or the lack of reserve which is possible at the golf club – we do not have to face continually the absence of all four states of privacy. In other institutions which resemble the security wing in certain aspects, large prisons, monasteries, convents, mental hospitals, there is usually some recognition given to these requirements of privacy even if the allowances which are made are still insufficient to prevent some suffering on the part of the inmates.

The lack of privacy of all kinds, and the particular nature of

11. Erving Goffman, *Stigma*, (Penguin, 1968).

the friendship patterns which exist in the wing have serious consequences for the men. There are few opportunities to assert individuality, to show personal autonomy, or to engage in orthodox types of emotional release. Problems of privacy and friendship converge in the area of sex, where careful group management is required to reduce tensions.

These prisoners are denied heterosexual relations for the whole of their sentence. They may see wives but not touch them. They may also as we have noted be forced into intimate dyadic relationships – relationships which as Roy said 'were just like marriage without the sex'. (On that occasion, a voice from the other side of the class reminded him, 'We can soon put that right.') We have not concentrated on this aspect of the men's lives in many of our discussions but they have not contradicted our assertion that homosexual involvement or the insulation of oneself from it constitute an important and even disturbing element in all their lives. Homosexuality in the wing has to be carefully regulated. There are those who try to contain it even in casual interaction, who press for it to be downgraded as a subject of conversation and it often appears only in the form of the defensive humour which occurs in most enforced all male settings.

The men are aware of the prison studies in which homosexual behaviour in prison is abandoned upon release and appear to view most such behaviour in the prison as only a temporary alternative to heterosexuality, a sexual variation which carries little stigma and which like masturbation is resorted to because of the circumstances. Moral indignation about the behaviour was completely absent, but there was some indication that although there was little disapproval of mutual masturbation, the 'insertee', the passive partner in anal intercourse was still regarded as a subject for ridicule and patronage. The point was not, however, that homosexuality was immoral but only that its presence amongst some but not all in the wing was an additional source of tension. Masturbation caused less problems. It was frequently resorted to in the wing, although we were told that it became increasingly difficult to 'get fantasies going' and we became aware of how dependent the men were upon magazines and books. Christmas was particularly looked forward to because of the promise of 'hard porn' being available. There was some individual anxiety about excessive masturbation. Prisoners talked of having 'been at it for hours' and relieved their concern by the usual comic references to 'going blind' and 'having it fall off'. Having a 'J. Arthur' was however generally recognized as a physical necessity; it was far from being an obsession. The presence of homosexual behaviour and masturbation in the wing also depended to some extent (although our evidence is contradictory here) upon the prison officers' readiness to tolerate some minor infringments of the security regulations and to permit the men a small degree of privacy.

Clearly sexual relationships in prison – as in outside society – are seldom just sexual and in a closed situation such as E-Wing they raised many other complex problems of daily interaction. Ordinary ways of coping with relationships might be quite inappropriate, as the following (part of a long chapter on homosexuality in a book of advice to political prisoners in federal penitentiaries) indicates:

It may seem strange at first but one must discipline oneself so as to ignore a large number of people with whom one is in close physical proximity. We mean that it is sometimes necessary to avert one's eyes from direct eye contact with other inmates and avoid visual as well as verbal communication. *Friendly attitudes just will not do.* [original italics] [12]

Homosexuality was not the only form of social behaviour which had to be regulated by the men, if there was to be some solidarity in the wing. The group also had to cope with the problem of emotional expression by individuals. The lack of privacy meant that there was nowhere to let off steam unobserved. The prison officers at Durham in the later period had become sensitive to this need. Louis reported: 'They allow

12. Howard Levy and David Miller, *Going to Jail: The Political Prisoner*, (New York, Grove Press, 1971), p. 149.

you to let off steam here – you can shout at the screw or look out of the windows at the screws below and shout – "Fuck off and take your fucking dogs with you".' But there was a need at times to put down other types of emotional expression which threatened the inmate group. One example dramatically illustrates the nature of such group regulation:

The men in the wing were allowed in the later period to prepare some of their own food. For this a selection of knives was made available. These were typically used by only one man – Louis – who organized most of the cooking. The arrival of a new and reputedly volatile inmate made the presence of knives in the wing a danger to everyone there. The situation was resolved by the organization of a rota system in which prisoners took it in turn to place themselves between the knives and the new inmate whenever Louis had to temporarily leave the scene. There were no incidents.

Nevertheless several of the major outbursts in the wing were in response to the conditions we have described in this chapter. But these were rarely individual. They were rather collective demonstrations by a group which at other times resorted to internal sanctioning in order that problems of privacy and sociability might in some way be moderated. Life may have been claustrophobic, incestuous, lacking in privacy; it may have generated anxieties about sex and aggression but at least a consciousness of these problems kept down the level of emotional reactions somewhat and ensured that some crude solidarity between a very diverse set of individuals was maintained.

We have been talking about the unnatural setting in E-Wing, about the lack of outside contacts, about the impossibility of making new friends. But, of course, it may be that to some extent our own visits and letters, our stress upon self-conscious recognition of such matters, constituted some relief for the prisoners with whom we regularly communicated. But our visits were occasional and we were fundamentally outsiders who walked out of the prison after a meeting. In any case there was the inevitable uncertainty amongst the men about what we were doing there in the first place, about whom we represented.

At first – as they told us – they often thought that we were there to discover their attitudes to the prison authorities or detect possible escape plans. We think that they came to accept our assurances to the contrary although – as they have remarked – we may simply be cleverer agents of social control than they have ever encountered before. After two weeks of discussing the ideology of spies, Paul, who had been reading most widely suddenly said: 'You know you say in joke, as a way of reassuring us, that you pass information to the Home Office? Well, Burgess and Maclean were always shouting about that they were passing secret information to Moscow – and they fucking were!'

CHAPTER FOUR

Time and deterioration

'Each minute may be marvellously – or horribly –
profound ... There are swift hours and very long
seconds. Past time is void. There is no chronology
of events to mark it; external duration no longer
exists.'

Victor Serge in *Men in Prison*

Many of the problems we discussed in the last chapter arose
from the claustrophobic nature of maximum security prisons.
These would be partially dispelled by the abolition of the
small security wing. As such abolition is the declared policy of
the Home Office, we may be accused of unfair concentration
upon a penal relic. After all, one security wing, Durham, has
already closed and the others are scheduled to go. There are
two answers to this charge which has been principally made by
our Home Office critics. In the first place we were concerned
with the problems of life in a unique environment. The fact
that the environment is about to be modified has as much
relevance to our study as had the imminent arrival of allied
troops to those studies concerned with the behaviour of people in
concentration camps. Then, the security wings have by no means
disappeared. As we write, the wings at Parkhurst, Leicester
and Chelmsford contain many of the men we knew at Durham
and contain them in such a way as to make the problems of
friendship and privacy we described in the last chapter just as
salient. Even when these security wings are closed, there is no
clear evidence that Category A men will mix with large numbers
of other prisoners. The six new dispersal prisons all contain
segregation units which are supposed to be reserved for emergency use in those cases where a prisoner causes particular
trouble in the main prison. There are, however, already indica-

tions at one dispersal prison that such units are being used as places in which Category A prisoners can be domiciled. This particular unit is becoming another prison within a prison, much like the traditional security wings we have already described. In one London prison an isolation unit is now being built which sounds very much like E-Wing.

Probably, though, some of the problems of friendship and privacy for long-term Category A men will be less acute after their dispersal from the orthodox security wings. But wherever the men spend the rest of their sentences – cooped up in the claustrophobic wings of Parkhurst or Leicester, or mixing freely with other men in the relatively open spaces of the new perimeter security prisons – they will have to contend with the problems of time and with fears of personal deterioration.

Time as a Problem

Time is a much more taken-for-granted element of everyday life than is friendship or privacy. We may periodically reflect upon our inability to manage without friends or privacy, we may talk philosophically about the need to seek new friends or dispense with old ones, and consciously reflect upon the merits of gregariousness and isolation. But behind such thinking and planning time ticks away relatively unobserved and unanalysed. We talk of it chiefly as a resource – we do not have enough of it, we cannot spare any for visits to our relations, we must make some so that we can squeeze in this or that activity. We can turn down any engagement on the grounds that we 'simply have no time' and we can become irritated by those who waste time or have time 'on their hands' without using it.

The association between time and money is hardly surprising in a highly industrialized society in which time wasted is often equivalent to money wasted in the great and continuing race for higher productivity. But there are occasions upon which the daily planning and allocation of intervals, the according of hours, days, and weekends to specific activities, breaks down. The sudden loss of a job, the cancellation of an engagement, removal from occupational time-scheduling by holiday or hospitalization, all provide opportunities for absenting ourselves from the obsession with marked time. It is then that time may become an open landscape rather than a set of pigeon-holes.

On these occasions 'past' and 'future' may have a meaning not in terms of time wasted or potential time to use in the future, but rather as parameters which define the present moment. Time then becomes less of an object in its own right. We then recognize that our past is not simply a pile of spent time, it has a personal meaning and significance. In the same way, the future becomes not simply a set of unfilled hours, but it is seen to hold a determinate position in our present existence. It assures us of the finiteness of life and thereby makes a mockery of the customary use of hours and days as steps towards some final goal. Our memory of the past and our recognition of the end of the future throw into relief our everyday human time-scheduling.

But such speculation is quickly ended for most of us. Life, as we say, catches up with us and we become locked back into the round of activities perhaps even persuading ourselves that only by such a self-conscious immersion can we manage to live at all. There is little consideration for those in our society who continually cast doubt upon the need to use time profitably. Much of the hostility felt towards such groups as hippies in contemporary society, is due to their disdain for conventional notions of time and their tendency to alter time perspectives by experiencing only the present and the immediate. One observer of the hippie subculture, Fred Davis,[1] notes how these groups raise doubts about 'the magically rationalistic faith in converting present efforts to future pay off', how their use of 'happenings' and interest in such ideas as astrology are attempts 'to denude the future of its temporal integrity – its unknowability and slow unfoldingness – by

1. Fred Davis, 'Why All of Us May Be Hippies Someday', *Trans-Action*, 5 December 1967.

fusing it indiscriminately with present dispositions and sensations'. He goes on:

The hippies' structureless round-of-day ('hanging loose'), his disdain for appointments, schedules, and straight society's compulsive parcelling out of minutes and hours, are all implicated in his intense reverence for the possibilities of the present and uninterest in the future. Few wear watches and as a colleague who has made a close participant observer study of one group of hippies remarked, 'None of them ever seems to know what time it is.'

Such experiences are, of course, linked in these subcultures with the use of mind-altering drugs and indeed a central claim made by proselytizers for such drugs concerns their properties for wholly altering time perspectives.[2] One subject in an L.S.D. experiment reports: 'One of the grossest distortions was that of time perception. Centuries were lived, yet the minute hand of the watch barely moved. My Rorschach took 200 light years, the longest on record.'[3]

Long-term prisoners do not volunteer like hippies for special time experiences, they are not briefly placed outside the normal routines of life like hospital patients or holiday makers, they have instead been given time as a punishment. But they have been given someone else's time. Their own time has been abstracted by the courts like a monetary fine and in its place they have been given prison time. This is no longer a resource but a controller. It has to be served rather than used. The men have described the ways in which they repeated their sentences to themselves – 'twenty years', 'thirty years' – in an attempt to understand the nature of their predicament.

Prisoners are, of course, not the only group who are forced to see time as a problem. For most workers, as one observer notes, '... Time is what the factory worker sells: not labour, not skill, but time, dreary time. Desolate factory time that passes so

2. For example, Timothy Leary, *The Politics of Ecstasy*, (London, Paladin, 1970).

3. Quoted in Sidney Cohen, *Drugs of Hallucination*, (London, Paladin, 1970), p. 86.

slowly compared with the fleeting seconds of the weekend.'[4] An industrial sociologist, Donald Roy, has provided a classic account of how a group of factory machine operatives kept themselves from 'going nuts' in a situation of monotonous work activity by a grim process of fighting against the clock.[5]

But the factory worker's day ends, he goes home, he has weekends and holidays, he will eventually retire. And although his time might indeed have been stolen from him he has not been sentenced to a long period in which he is continually and inevitably plunged into considerations about the meaning of time. A long prison sentence is not, however, a short intermission in the real business of life, it is the real business of life.

In these circumstances it is not surprising that the most frequently used metaphor to describe prison experience is a temporal one: serving a sentence is 'doing time' and the most frequent injunction to inmates is to 'do your time and not let your time do you':

In prison, time accumulates a new dimension. You try to eat it away rather than enjoy it. If a prisoner is having difficulty with his station, if the days are hopelessly long, he is doing 'hard time'. Instead of asking why another is making life difficult one asks 'why are you cutting into my time?' And a frequent answer when one tells of his troubles is 'do your own time' or 'don't press my time'.[6]

The Present and the Future

Those who dislike speculation about past and future, can usually see an end to the situation which has induced such reflective breaks in the normal scheduling of life; they can consider plans for when they get out of hospital, or prison, or home on holiday. There are still bills to be paid, visits to

4. Ronald Fraser (ed.), *Work*, (Penguin, 1968), vol. I, p. 12).
5. Donald Roy, '"Banana Time": Job Satisfaction and Informal Interaction,' *Human Organization*, 18, (1959–60).
6. John Rosevear, 'The Fourth Mad Wall' in Ross Firestone (ed.) *Getting Busted*, (New York, Douglas Books, 1970), p. 234.

relations to be arranged, home-coming parties to be organized during those times when one is absent from the normal run of life. The ordinary temporal scheduling of one's affairs is kept in the background of one's mind by the continued operation of such financial, domestic and social matters. When twenty years of one's time is taken away, even these routine matters disappear. The landscape of time, the past and the future, and the actual significance of the present moment insistently occupy the mind. The prisoners in E-Wing found Victor Serge's description of this obsessive state the most accurate.

The unreality of time is palpable. Each second falls slowly. What a measureless gap from one hour to the next. When you tell yourself in advance that six months – or six years – are to pass like this, you feel the terror of facing an abyss. At the bottom, mists in the darkness.[7]

This unlimited time does not have the same subjective appeal for the prisoners as for the hippie drug user, or the monk or hermit. For as we have said it is not their own time. They did not volunteer for twenty years' self-reflection. And neither do they have a ready-made set of interpretations, a personal ideology to fill the hours of self-reflection. The sophisticated drug-user may be self-consciously using his expanded consciousness of time to construct mental reveries, the hermit and the monk may be conversing with God in their time-free trances, but the long-term prisoner has no such ready-made mystical voyages to take the place of his previous involvement in plans, schedules and routines.

In these circumstances, it is not surprising that the prisoners live for the present – not from some ideological disdain for future planning, but out of necessity. To quote from the experience

7. Victor Serge, *Men In Prison*, (London, Gollancz, 1970, p. 56). It was not only here that the prisoners found Victor Serge most accurate. In our view, *Men in Prison* is the best existing account of survival and resistance in prisons and we have been consistently stimulated by its insights.

of one American prisoner: 'You do your time in little daily jerks, living from one microscopic pleasure to the next – from breakfast pancakes to a flash of blue sky . . . Try it any other way and you'll be pounding the walls, screaming until your lungs give out.'[8] Richard Byrd, isolated in a polar camp, came to the same solution:

> I built a wall between myself and the past in an effort to extract every ounce of diversion and creativeness inherent in my immediate surroundings. Every day I experimented with new schemes for increasing the content of the hours . . . My environment was intrinsically treacherous and difficult but I saw ways to make it agreeable. I tried to cook more rapidly, take weather and auroral observations more expertly and do routine things more systematically. Full mastery of the impinging moment was my goal.[9]

In prison, one also has to find ways of 'increasing the content of the hours' but 'mastery of the impinging moment' has a very different meaning for those who – unlike explorers or even short-term prisoners – do not have a clear conception of the future after one survives the treacherous environment. It is all very well to engage in relatively 'meaningless' activities – such as making weather observations – so long as this can be seen as part of a finite period of waiting before release. The long-termer has only the choice between surrendering himself to this meaningless world as a life project or obsessionally thinking about the future – a near certain way of doing hard time.

This discussion leads us to the paradox inherent in the way long-termers deal with the future. In one sense the future is unthinkable. Roy once remarked that, 'If I really thought that I had to do another seventeen years, I'd do myself in.' Other prisoners fight attempts by prison officers to bring home the time factor. Jock said: 'Whenever a screw asks me how long do I think I'll do, I always say, "Oh, about thirty-five years", because then he can get no advantage from the conversation. If I

8. J. Godwin, *Alcatraz: 1938–1963*, (New York, Doubleday & Co., 1963).

9. Richard Byrd, *Alone*, (London, Putnam, 1938), p. 109.

say, "Twenty," he'd say, "Oh no, I think it'll be at least twenty-five." Really I don't know what any of the figures mean.' The paradox arises in that while the men reject attempts by others to raise the subject, or dismiss thoughts about the nature of the future from their own minds, they are also relying upon ideas about a future life outside to sustain themselves through their temporally undifferentiated days.

For without entertaining the prospect of a life beyond the prison, without literally believing in an 'after life', one has to either face the fact that one's life was over at the moment of entering the prison, or that one's life is that existence which takes place within the prison. The concept of 'my life' is an important one in our culture. Young men look ahead to life, old men look back upon it. People talk about their life being behind or ahead of them. In other words we identify life with particular periods of our existence, with the time between youth and old age, that time before prison, the time which is to come after prison. What appears to be totally unacceptable is the idea that one's life is experienced in prison. One may be serving life, but one is not serving 'my life'. This was certainly true for the men we knew and Farber found it to be the case in his interviews with 'Eight Men Whose Chances of Ever Getting Out Are Slight'. His principal generalization was that '*in not a single case of these men whose chances of ever getting out are negligible is there complete resignation to dying in prison.* That most dismal of all platitudes "Where there is life there's hope" takes on a new freshness.'[10] (Italics in original.)

Marking Time

In the circumstances, prisoners who have to sustain their lives in some way look around for ways of marking out the passage of the days, ways of differentiating and dividing time. Psychologists and sociologists have paid little attention to the problems

10. Maurice Farber, 'Suffering and Time Perspective of the Prisoner', p. 180.

which occur for those whose lives are suddenly emptied of time markers in this total way. Perhaps their involvement in a particularly highly scheduled career structure makes them insensitive to the empty formless years which others have to occupy. At least the only major research into such matters was carried out by Julius Roth, a sociologist who suddenly found himself absorbed by the problem of time-scheduling when he was away from academic life and spending time as a patient in a T.B. sanatorium.[11]

Patients who enter such sanatoria are often surprised to find that they are given no exact date for their release. Lack of information over this matter leads to a frantic activity. Doctors, nurses and other patients are repeatedly questioned and quite ambiguous items of information are treated as significant clues. The demand for a timetable leads the patients to bargain with physicians about the nature and extent of their improvement in order that an earlier release date may be negotiated. Roth's principal concern is to indicate how important career timetables are in most areas of life and to demonstrate the concern which arises when the stages which constitute them are ambiguous or non-existent.

This study by Roth brings out the fact that one obvious benchmark, one way of dividing time, which is built into the sanatorium régimes, is the notion of linear progress. One gets better or stronger; one is able to do things one could not do before. But in E-Wing no such reference to linear progress is possible. Criteria for the positive evaluation of one's progress are not built into the system, and there are no progressive stages of reward and punishment. Though parole is a reward somewhat contingent on good behaviour, most of the men we know see its attainment (realistically) as so remote that it hardly functions as a stage of progress. Indeed, the chances of parole can be almost arbitrarily affected by the sudden appearance of a newspaper item on a notorious criminal. The men in the wing saw any popular reference to them in the Sunday newspapers as setting back even further their chances of remission.

11. Julius Roth, *Timetables*, (Indianapolis, Bobbs-Merrill, 1962).

They were sophisticated enough to know how much the deliberations of a parole board were eventually influenced by public opinion, despite its avowed concern with the actual individual under consideration.

Unlike the T.B. patients described by Roth, these men have no opportunities for bargaining with the authorities. Their behaviour cannot influence their timetable, there is no room for 'making deals' with their keepers that will help to shorten the stretch or bring an earlier relaxation of restrictions. Unlike hospitals, again, there is nothing in the behaviour of the staff to give the prisoners any clues about when events should occur in the passage of time. The absence and the inscrutability of the Home Office personnel who control a few of the temporal and situational outcomes, are seen as necessary ways of keeping control and preserving security.

The men therefore tend to create stages themselves. They build their own subjective clock in order to protect themselves from the terror of 'the misty abyss'. There are a few achievements which can be used to mark the passage of time. One can engage in mind-building (reading or studying) and in body-building (usually weightlifting). Some of the men talk about an educational career, describing the passage from 'O' levels to 'A' levels to university with an enthusiasm which is rarely found in even those who have a chance of occupationally capitalizing upon the restricted years of specialized study which constitute contemporary secondary education. The significance of weightlifting in this context may be less than we at first thought. It was possible in the wing to find men who agreed that being able to lift extra weights constituted a way of marking out improvements over time, but a somewhat more cynical view came in reply to an article of ours in which we had made this point. An ex-member of the class wrote: 'In my opinion body-building was a bad example because it serves far more potent motives than the need for a concrete progression. Some of the prisoners in question would rather put an inch on their biceps than take a year off their sentence.'

In any case there is a danger in these pursuits of mental and physical targets, for there soon comes a day in which progress is inhibited, in which fewer books are read, fewer essays written and less weights lifted. In normal life we can declare that our interests have declined in such matters and re-invest successfully in foreign travel and golf. For these prisoners the loss of such matters marks the re-entry of unstructured time.

There are other methods of marking time. One can tick off certain fixed, definable periods: days, weeks or months. But this may merely bring home the unreality of time even more forcibly. As Serge writes:

So as not to lose track of the date, you have to count the days attentively, mark each one with a cross. One morning you discover that there are forty-seven days – or one hundred and twenty, or three hundred and forty-seven! – and that it is a straight path leading backwards without the slightest break: colourless, insipid, senseless. Not a single landmark is visible. Months have passed like so many days; entire days pass like minutes. Future time is terrifying. The present is heavy with torpor.

Each minute may be marvellously – or horribly – profound. That depends to a certain extent on yourself. There are swift hours and very long seconds. Past time is void. There is no chronology of events to mark it; external duration no longer exists.[12]

It is the lack of a chronology of events that is most important in Serge's description. Of course, days come and go, but they do not pass as they do on the outside when one is waiting for an event, simply because they are no longer beads on a wire, or counters on a board. They are not progressively used up as one moves toward a goal. They are isolated entities, existing away from the normal cumulative linear context they inhabit. In Roth's words: 'The life prisoner can look forward to Sunday as a welcome break in a dreary routine, but the succession of Sundays does not lead him anywhere.'[13]

12. Victor Serge, *Men in Prison*, pp. 56–7.
13. Julius Roth, *Timetables*, p. 99.

In these circumstances, the external clock may be partially abandoned in favour of such subjective markers as changes in mood or feeling. These may have a reality and a temporal meaning which is lacking in the world of clocks and diaries and calendars. Christopher Burney although writing specifically about solitary confinement, captures this transition:

Days in prison are distinguishable only by such rare incidents as from time to time make one of them memorable among its fellows. Although I never lost count of the week or of the date, I followed them subconsciously, and life was divided into longer periods, limited by a state of mind or a physical condition; and it was these more personal symbols than sun or moon which marked out the calendar.[14]

Shorter sentences undoubtedly are managed in more orthodox ways: days are crossed off calendars and hours until release are pencilled on all walls. The techniques for conducting such time management become accepted parts of prison folk-lore. Leary recalls noticing that the numbers pinned to a trustee's wall signifying the date were removed each day but there was no number for the day on which he was looking at the wall. He asked the prisoner why and the reply was: 'in con terminology when you wake up in the morning that day is over'.[15] There were attempts to advocate variations in such techniques to meet the case of long sentences. When Roland arrived in E-Wing he turned to Paul for advice on the structuring of time. 'How am I going to do twenty years?' Paul, on the basis of three years' experience of an equally long sentence, provided the only reassurance he knew: 'It's easy, do it five years at a time.'

There are of course the 'incidents' referred to by Burney which occur in the wing and which break up the dull passage of time. Many of these are, however, unscheduled and it is

14. Christopher Burney, *Solitary Confinement*, (New York, Coward & McCann, 1952), p. 23.

15. Timothy Leary, *Jail Notes*, (New York, Douglas Books, 1970), p. 77.

therefore not possible to look forward to them or prepare for them. The sudden transfer of a man from the wing or the arrival of a new inmate is typically unexpected. Events which occur in this sudden way are deprived of significance. Once again it is easy to forget how important for our existence is the anticipation of such matters in everyday life. The dull Monday morning becomes acceptable because of the promise of an evening out on Thursday, the long winter is bearable because of an anticipated Easter holiday. Each event by itself may be trivial, even dispensable without great psychic cost, but together they constitute a set of inducements which help to move us forward through time.

Donald Roy's factory workers, spending a day of 'infinitesimal cerebral excitation', repetitively clocking a machine, faced similar problems of marking time: the lunch break, occasional trips to the lavatory or drinking fountain, obviously functioned to 'break the day up into digestible parts'. But Roy soon realized that the men were doing more than this, they were creating 'incidents' and in fact much of their informal activity was devoted to deliberately making new time markers and interruptions in the 'day's long grind'. These were not *just* rest pauses or work interruptions or accentuations of progress points in the passage of time – although they performed this latter function better than a clock:

If the daily series of interruptions be likened to a clock then the comparison might best be made with a special kind of cuckoo clock, one with a cuckoo which can provide variation in its announcements and can create such an interest in them that the intervening minutes become filled with intellectual content. ... The group interactions thus not only marked off the time; they gave it content and hurried it along.[16]

The clicker operators called these breaks 'times' and they usually involved the consumption of food or drink: coffee time, peach time, banana time, fish time or coke time. All the themes

16. Donald Roy, ' "Banana Time": Job Satisfaction and Informal Interaction', p. 162.

in the group's interactions, their joking, horseplay, ritualistic conversation provided interaction which captured attention and held interest to make the long day pass.

The routine of E-Wing was so short of events that even our classes became something of an occasion. We were told by the men, quite self-consciously (gently mocking themselves and us at the same time) how they would sometimes make quite elaborate preparations – like 'dressing up' – for our meetings. We were at least outsiders and this they found reassuring. We could pass on in detail the changes in life which were occurring outside, we could interpret changes in the political climate, in drug use, in popular music, in sexual permissiveness. Their ability to assimilate these changes, to approve or accept the widespread use of marihuana or the increased permissiveness of the cinema, provided some type of guarantee that they could rejoin society without too great a strain upon their release. To put it pretentiously, we helped to keep them in gear with external time and in this way provided them with a way of marking time which did not simply refer to the unserved years of their sentence.

But our visits did not of course have the emotional significance or impact of visits from friends and relatives. Such visits were events to be planned for, to be anticipated over days and weeks. Fred Davis talks about the 'accordion effect' that such events produce: a man stretches the time of the event, from the point of its anticipation through to the discussions that follow its occurrence.[17] With more feeling Serge calls these effects 'exultation': the radiant joy at the expectation of recognition by others, and the fact that 'a fifteen-minute visit is enough to fill long days with expectation and long days with meaning afterwards'.

Unfortunately, as we noted in the last chapter, such events may become increasingly rare as the prisoner moves towards the end of his first decade inside. The joy produced by a visit

17. Quoted by Kathy Calkins in 'Time: Perspectives, Marking and Styles of Usage', *Social Problems 17*, 6 (Spring 1970).

and the structuring of time which its anticipation allows is not enough to overcome the pains of anxiety which a possible break in that relationship induces.[18]

Work and Making Time Pass

Victor Serge described the 'present' in prison as being 'heavy with torpor'. Days do not go past at their conventional pace. However the adoption of new methods of time-scheduling in this ambiguous situation is not the only problem facing the long-termer. It is not just the division of time which concerns him but the *speed* of its passage. How can it be made to go more quickly? The anticipation of visits or the expectation of letters does nothing about increasing the speed at which time goes. Obsessional concern with such future events may even slow time as anyone who has fixedly waited for a kettle to boil will know.

18. We should mention in passing one of the solutions some prison reformers and many of the E-Wing men themselves have suggested as a way of alleviating some of the pains associated with very long sentences. This is to introduce some measure of indeterminacy in which the men's release or parole would depend on progress within the prison – 'progress' being assessed by evidence of good behaviour and willingness to change. Experience with such systems, however, suggests that only new temporal problems will result. In California, for example, the Indeterminate Sentence (IS) was introduced for a number of humanitarian motives, for example, to allow rehabilitative considerations rather than purely legal retribution to determine the time a man spent inside. The results of this system have been anything but humane, and under these conditions the obsession with time only increases. To the administrator, time becomes a weapon and means of control. The staff use the impending hearing before the review board as a manipulative device to ensure passivity and obedience to the régime. For the inmate who 'gets a date' of release time acquires a new and positive meaning. But if a date is denied, time perspectives are shattered: the inmate has to restructure his temporal strategies because of the uncertainty, to change his expectations of the future and to employ further frustrating efforts in attempting to discover his fate. (This footnote makes use of unpublished research by Marty Miller on the temporal strategies used by prisoners serving indeterminate sentences in California.)

In everyday life we typically make time go by throwing our-selves into occupational activities. We bury ourselves in our work so that we have no time for 'clock-watching'. This method is not much use even to the average prisoner. It is not much use hoping that a man in Parkhurst's 'tag shop' will become involved in his job of sticking metal ends in to the lengths of green string used to keep files together. It is even less reasonable to suppose that men facing twenty years in jail can lose themselves in repairing sewing machines or making mosquito nets – to name two of the jobs provided for E-Wing men. But people faced with such monotonous jobs in the outside world do, of course, cope. One commentator on the workers' struggle to 'cling to the remnants of joy in work' notes that 'it is psychologically impossible to deprive any kind of work of all its positive emotional elements'.[19] The worker will always find *some* meaning, some scope for initiative, play and creative impulse in the activity assigned to him.

We doubt that this is true for long-term prisoners. The cul-turally defined meanings of work: learning a trade, making something for one's family, financial incentive are gone. Even if prison jobs were interesting, work for a life prisoner has a very peculiar status indeed: if factory workers have to desperately invest jobs with meaning and time markers, then prisoners without clear meanings or time markers have to try and find them in the work they are given. So their problem is a double one.

In these circumstances it is not surprising to find that only five men out of the forty-two in the Eccleston sample listed work as a way of making time go faster. Ten of the rest saw no ways at all of solving this problem and the others mentioned hobbies, reading, or private study: activities we would regard in the outside world as leisure. When workshops were introduced into E-Wing in 1968 there were references to the fact that the men had done no work for six months and were becoming lazy. Certainly many of them regarded the in-troduction of the workshops as an additional punishment rather

19. Henri de Man, quoted in Donald Roy, op. cit., p. 160.

than as an escape from torpor and this was the main reason for the protest and barricade which immediately followed. An editorial comment at this time admitted that the work that was being offered was not interesting or relevant. The real value of the new workshops was that they would 'occupy idle hands and minds, and perpetuate the idea that work, as opposed to idleness, is a requirement of life'. (*Newcastle Journal.*)

The very use of the word 'work' is misleading in this context. As Erving Goffman observed in *Asylums*:

In the ordinary arrangements of living in our society, the authority of the work place stops with the worker's receipt of a money payment; the spending of this in a domestic and recreational setting is the worker's private affair and constitutes a mechanism through which the authority of the work place is kept within strict bounds. But to say that inmates of total institutions have their full day scheduled for them is to say that all their essential needs will have to be planned for. Whatever the incentive given for work, then, this incentive will not have the structural significance it has on the outside. There will have to be different motives for work and different attitudes toward it. This is a basic adjustment required of the inmates and of those who must induce them to work.[20]

The absurdity of 'work' within the context of the security wing is perhaps most neatly illustrated by the fact that what is a 'job' in one wing – making soft toys – is offered as a hobby in another.

We always found it difficult to maintain a conversation about work with prisoners in E-Wing. They gave the impression that there were other more important matters to be discussed. What job they were doing at the time made little apparent difference to their feelings about life inside. Once again, we are able to turn to Farber for some interesting confirmation of these findings. With the help of prison officials and prisoners he divided up jobs along a good-bad axis and then checked on the the relationship between the relative suffering experienced by

20. Erving Goffman, *Asylums*, (Penguin, 1969), p. 10.

the prisoners and the quality of the job. There was no link at all. Those with bad jobs suffered no more or less than those with good. He was sufficiently surprised by this result to check up on job satisfaction as well. For perhaps men who had good jobs might *dislike* them and vice versa. But no relationship between degree of job satisfaction and suffering could be found. Farber concludes by saying that 'what would seem to be one of the most important of day-to-day activities bears no relation to suffering. Suffering is related to broader, less immediate aspects of the life situation.'[21]

We have been a little too sweeping, however, in writing off work as a way of speeding up the passage of time. There are a few in prison who feel it to be better than nothing. They admit that it is a self-deception, but claim that there is no alternative. They feel sympathetic to Ivan Denisovich's view: 'How time flew when you were working. That was something he'd often noticed. The days rolled by in the camp – they were over before you could say "knife". But the years never rolled by, they never moved by a second.'[22]

For some time we assumed that these differences in attitude towards the use of work to pass time were idiosyncratic. But behind the cynical view of work may lie a concern about what is involved in passing time in this way. It was the more rebellious members of the group who played down the significance of becoming involved in such activities. In doing this they may have been recognizing the loss of personal autonomy which is involved in fitting oneself to others' schedules. Kathy Calkins, who has conducted a very sensitive investigation into the significance of time in a rehabilitation hospital, reserves the phrase 'time passing' for this particular style of adaptation:

When time is *passed* (our stress), the patient tends to relinquish a certain amount of control over his own time. Essentially, he

21. Maurice Farber in K. Lewin (ed.), *Studies in Authority and Frustration*, p. 174.
22. Alexander Solzhenitsyn, *One Day in the Life of Ivan Denisovich*, (Penguin, 1968).

fits into the time of others according to their time prescriptions. In this style, the patient voluntarily fills pockets of time outlined by the institution.[23]

For the long-termer to seek to pass time by immersing himself in institutional routines may be to accord some type of legitimacy to the institution. It is to acknowledge that his sentence will be served in accordance with the intentions of the authorities.

The marking and the passing of time are then major elements in long-term prisoners' lives. Time presents itself as a problem. It is no longer a resource to be used, but rather an object to be contemplated – an undifferentiated landscape which has to be marked out and traversed. Conventional markers cannot be used and neither can one's journey be expedited by recourse to conventional methods. Nevertheless the length of the journey continually preoccupies the mind, for only after it has been made, can life be effectively resumed.

There is another preoccupation for these particular time travellers. As the journey proceeds they are accompanied by a number of growing anxieties. Above all long-term prisoners have to learn to live with a constant fear of deterioration.

The Fear of Deterioration

When Roy arrived to start his twenty-five-year sentence some screws tried to reassure him. 'Look at Dawson,' they said, pointing to the top landing, 'he's been in for nearly twenty years and he's perfectly content.' Roy would not accept this consolation: 'How could I know if he was content? Anyway what was he content *about*?' Roy's fear was that he might lapse into a state of contentment which marked a departure from reality, but which he did not recognize as such.

The long-term prisoners all felt like this. Over the years

23. Calkins, 'Time: Perspectives, Marking and Styles of Usage', p. 495.

they have asked us to comment on any signs of deterioration we observed, to record their personality changes, to discuss their cultural inadequacies and their social maladjustments. Not that we are really needed to point out any signs of deterioration. The men we have met are only too ready to do it for each other. One evening they all sat discussing the future programme for the class. The regular group was trying to decide the best dates for a new set of lectures. 'Well, Stan's here on Friday,' said Paul. 'Monday,' said Roy, 'today's Friday, *you're going*.' 'I'm not – anybody could make that mistake. My mother gets the days mixed. There's nothing special about that.'

The incident is trivial but it indicates the obsessive concern with signs of deterioration and the self-consciousness with which such fears were faced. These men felt that all around them were examples of people who had turned into cabbages because they had not been sufficiently vigilant. Every day they encountered an old sex offender who spent hours merely cleaning and filling the teapot, a mindless activity which the old man appeared to be contented with. And this was their problem: at what price would they achieve peace of mind and contentment? Would they start behaving like the old man, as a way of banishing the ghosts of time, the fear of deterioration and not knowing what was happening to them? In other words, would the cumulative result of years of working at something which looked like adaptation, in fact really be a process of learning how to deteriorate?

We stress again the learning element and the meaning the men assign to their situation. The sensory deprivation studies we briefly reviewed in Chapter Two refer to behavioural effects such as hallucinations, perceptual distortions and mood changes. Studies of institutions such as mental hospitals and prisons have repeatedly shown effects variously described as institutional neurosis, regression and apathy. Even in a prison with many short-termers, Terence and Pauline Morris found that the two years of their research was 'sufficient to observe several prisoners on the downhill path, men who made fewer and fewer jokes, whose appearance became increasingly untidy and who became progressively uninterested in everything around them'.[24]

But in all these studies we must remember that the situation changes once the subjects are aware of what is happening. This changes the meaning of the experience, it allows the person to evaluate it in terms of his conception of himself. Central to this conception was the wish to be the same person on leaving prison as on arrival. Bettelheim recorded the presence of this wish in his concentration camp study. The inmate there wanted 'to safeguard his ego in such a way that, if by any good luck he should regain liberty, he would be approximately the same person he was when deprived of liberty.'[25]

An immediate difficulty for the long-term prisoner who adopts this hope arises from the forced changes in self-conception which the initial imprisonment imposes. Goffman and others have described in detail the systematic ways in which entry to a total institution involves a series of assaults upon the self which have the effect of contradicting or failing to corroborate previous self-conceptions. We would not wish to make too much of these degradation ceremonies here. The men we knew had mostly been to prison before and were unlikely to be intimidated by prison staff whom they regarded as their intellectual and social inferiors. They did not like the loss of their hair, their clothes and their possessions, but it would be inaccurate to describe them as typically mortified by such forms of disfigurement. Their self-conception was more critically challenged by other members of the wing. However notorious the person had been on the outside, whatever his press coverage, there was a persistent debunking which occurred when he took his place with the other prisoners. Exploits were likely to be described in disparaging terms – they were not endowed with the degree of skill or organization which was accorded to them outside by the mass media.

24. Terence and Pauline Morris, *Pentonville, A Sociological Study of An English prison*, p. 165.

25. Bruno Bettelheim, *The Informed Heart*, (New York, Free Press of Glencoe, 1960), p. 3.

But once this compromise had been effected, allowances were made for idiosyncrasies. Indeed, there was a self-conscious tendency to tolerate such idiosyncrasies, in that they were recognized as indicative of the particular character of the person and were therefore deserving of some respect in an environment which appeared geared to the planing down of any distinctive personality traits.

There were two principal ways in which these men set about maintaining their self-conception. They either fought back or engaged in a retreatism.

We deal with the distribution of these styles of adaptation in E-Wing at a later point – concentrating particularly on the diverse styles of fighting back. These range from planning escapes to engaging in long-drawn battles with the authorities; they are all attempts to pit the self against others.

Retreatism or resignation is, however, perhaps more generally thought of as the lifer's adaptation. Certainly in the Eccleston sample there was evidence of resignation. Although the thirty-two men interviewed had only served an average of a third of their sentences, one half declared themselves completely resigned to their predicament. The typical inmate in this group shows some of the characteristics of 'situational withdrawal' as described by Goffman. He 'withdraws apparent attention from everything except events immediately around his body and sees these in a perspective not employed by others present'.[26] These prisoners wanted to be left alone – by the authorities and by other prisoners. One was asked: 'What do you miss?' He replied, 'Nothing really. But I see others go for visits – one day I'll go as well.' Another prisoner when asked to design the perfect prison could only suggest that modern continuous floors might be used instead of a balcony. One of the prisoners who conducted the interviews described the withdrawn nature of a member of this group as 'the type you could put in a field and still find him there in the morning'. These prisoners cooperated with the authorities in the interests of a quiet life, they were at the opposite end of the continuum

26. Erving Goffman, *Asylums*, p. 61.

to the 'cowboys', one of whom when questioned about his readiness to get help from the authorities simply said, 'Fuck them – I would *ask* for *nothing*!'

Of course some element of resignation must be present among all long-termers, but we don't know how many of those who declare themselves to be resigned had consciously adopted this attitude or whether it had somehow overtaken them.

However, we know that in E-Wing those who adopt a policy of retreatism calculatedly allow themselves to become interested in work, they decide to go along with the routine. 'Eat your porridge every day/and do your bird the easy way' is their motto. Roy felt that this technique was the only possible one. The idea of struggling in any way for another seventeen years struck him as absurd. Any resistance to the institution which remained for Roy consisted almost entirely of his knowledge that he had decided to go along with it. This meant, in principle at least, that at any moment he could reverse that decision. But if those who struggle find themselves tiring as they observe the irrelevance of their studies, the failure of their escapes, or the futility of their campaigns, those who deliberately retreat have to face the awful fact that their stress upon the self-consciousness of their adaptation may be no more than a verbal cloak which masks a complete capitulation to the system and an abandonment of a previously held self-image. Everyone recognizes that after a few years the problem becomes more intense.

Victor Serge is again the writer who 'says the right things' as far as most of these men are concerned. He traces the deterioration in prisoners which follows the initial period of struggle. This initial period 'varies in length, and ends, once a man is free from a decisive mental aberration and no longer puts up much resistance, in a state of vegetative slow-motion existence in which sharp sufferings and sharp joys no longer play a part'. At this point, says Serge, the prisoners give in to morbid lewdness, to hate, to superstitions and to obsessions about 'their case', their few possessions and their possible death. He cruelly adds that these men 'will die in prison. For the fear of death is already death's lure.'[27]

The possibility of turning into the type of vegetable Serge describes haunts these men. Will they still have feelings when they come out, will they be able to think and talk? David, characteristically, reduces the terror of these questions by humorously staring them in the face: 'The vain attempt to stay the hand of time is an obsession with us here. We're always telling each other how fit we'll be when we're released. The septuagenarian who marries his nineteen year old secretary is a symbol of hope; we gloss over the fact that his personal appeal is amplified by a string of hotels and oil wells. We believe to a man that young girls like mature men.'

We have not known these men long enough to make any generalizations about how they will deteriorate. It seems, however, that many of the men already suffer from what R. D. Laing has called 'ontological insecurity'.[28] This term describes the state in which one doubts the integrity of self, the reliability of natural processes and the substantiality of others. In some forms this insecurity can take the form of a dread of the 'possibility of turning, or being turned, from a live person into a dead thing, into a stone, into a robot, an automaton, without personal autonomy of action, an *it* without subjectivity'.

We said before that the men in the wings could see around them examples of what they might become in twenty years. Most security prisons have a handful of inmates who have been inside for very long periods and whose survival is part of the folk culture of the institution, passed on to each new group of prisoners. The American prison system has thrown up some remarkable cases such as Nathan Leopold[29] (of the Leopold and Loeb murder case in the twenties) and the legendary Robert Stroud (the Birdman of Alcatraz) who served periods of forty or fifty years with little apparent deterioration. We know too

27. Victor Serge, *Men in Prison*, p. 58.
28. R. D. Laing, *The Divided Self*, (Penguin, 1965), p. 46.
29. See Nathan Leopold, *Life + 99 Years*, (London, Gollancz, 1958).

little about these people to understand how they survived – although their presence suggests that there is no fixed point beyond which the prisoner inevitably cracks. In a book about their experiences in the Indiana State prison, some inmates have described the very different fates of two long-termers.[30] Both had been inside for over forty years. One had apparently put his time to 'good use' by working hard at self-improvement and education. Of the other, one of his fellows writes:

His blue eyes are watery and vacant, focused on some faraway scene that is real only in the deep recess of his mind. He sits in the sun and recalls another era. He makes us uncomfortable. He is a man apart from his fellow men, a stranger to the world outside prison walls. Long ago he was caught up in the dreary monotony of prison life. Now in his failing years even prison life has passed him by . . . he relates only to prison events: when they . . . added the extra fifteen feet to the prison wall; when they enforced the lock step; when they released Dillinger . . . This old man is our badge of helplessness.

We know little about the range of adaptations after fifteen or twenty years in prison have passed. Those E-Wing men who had been inside for years only occasionally attended our classes. Only one of them (who had served fourteen years) came regularly and wrote to us afterwards in a moving way about his state of retreatism:

Can you imagine what it is like being a prisoner for life, your dreams turn into nightmares and your castles to ashes, all you think about is fantasy and in the end you turn your back on reality and live in a contorted world of make-believe, you refuse to accept the rules of fellow mortals and make ones that will fit in with your own little world, there is no daylight in this world of the 'lifer', it is all darkness, and it is in this darkness that we find peace and the ability to live in a world of our own, a world of make-believe.

30. H. Jack Griswold et al., *An Eye For An Eye*, (New York, Pocket Books, 1971, Chapter 7).

When we read this extract (with his permission) to the rest of the class, David and Roy fought hard against its pessimism – complaining that despite its literary flow it was an example of defeatism – a defeatism which could not be allowed and which must be actively fought against. They recognized their psychic enemy within the writing and were anxious to root him out. But neither they nor we know whether the reaction described in the letter was merely the idiosyncratic solution of one lifer or whether – and more terrifyingly – it represented the typical psychic environment in which most long-termers will eventually find themselves. The terrible fear is that one may be overtaken by resignation, by a desire for death, however much one consciously resists. As one prisoner told Victor Serge:

My intellect . . . has not faltered; but it has grown dim. I have never resigned myself; but resignation has entered me, has bent me down to the ground and told me: 'Rest'. To tell the truth, I'm not sure it didn't tell me: 'Die slowly.'[31]

31. Victor Serge, *Men in Prison*, p. 170.

CHAPTER FIVE

History, authority and solidarity

'I remember there was a good screw at one place . . .
he died!'

David

The picture we have painted in the last two chapters misses
out some very important elements of life in E-Wing. The
problems of marking time, of making and breaking friends, of
finding privacy and avoiding contamination are all real enough
but they do not exist against an undifferentiated background.
E-Wing is not just a stark empty environment in which problems are encountered and resolved with varying degrees of
success. It is, as we showed in Chapter One, a place with its
own history, with a distinctive cultural tradition, a tradition
which informs present attitudes and behaviour. In addition –
as we argue in Chapter Seven – behaviour in the wing must be
understood in terms of the biographies of its members and the
ideologies which inform their adaptations.

Though men may well be aware of the irrelevance of their
personal past when they are faced with an apparently never-
ending sentence, they nevertheless are aware as a group of the
meaning of the history of the wing for their present predicament. And while very involved in personal problems, they still
recognize that they are part of a community which shares
historically accumulated attitudes and beliefs about the prison,
the wing, the guards and the governor. To attempt to understand their reactions to prison life in the wing without knowing
about such matters is equivalent to attempting to explain the
reactions of industrial workers to their present predicament by
relying upon an analysis of their contemporary circumstances.

In prisons, as in any factory, the present level of consciousness can only be understood by reference to the series of historical situations in which it has been developed.

What exactly are these historical situations? We have described some of them in the opening chapter of this book – the founding of the wing, the riots, the barricades. But this was what we called the 'public' history of the wing. Our familiarity with this type of history at first made us insensitive to the significance of the 'private' history. Rather like nineteenth-century colonialists we were surprised by the presence of an indigenous history, by the men's sense of a cultural continuity which linked together past events in the wing, even though they might not have personally been involved in them. The particular history of E-Wing informs the contemporary consciousness of its members in a very immediate sense, for unlike non-prisoners who belong to a variety of organizations each with its own history, these men have no alternatives to consider. This means that memories of such localized phenomena as the riot or the hunger strike are dominant elements in the collective contemporary definition of the situation. The repetition and elaboration of such stories gives them legendary status and helps to shape later action.

The principal theme which runs through historical accounts of the wing is the gradual assertion of control by the prisoners. Initially the wing was designed to be maximally secure and maximally repressive. The prisoners who were sent there were as powerless as the authorities could make them. Gradually however, objective changes occurred in their situation. There may have been some high-level decision to modify the conditions, but this is not the reason one finds the prisoners articulating. For them their gains, the gradual increments of autonomy, were wrested from the authorities by a series of planned campaigns.

We suspect that the belief that they have gained some concessions is realistic, although they can hardly be said to have gained much control over their environment. As Roy wrote to one of us recently, his freedom is that of Beckett's slave: 'to crawl eastward along the deck of a westward moving ship'.

But even such limited freedom was the result of a struggle. The self-consciousness of this struggle and its evolutionary nature cannot be better expressed than in the following account by Chris which was given to us as a corrective to a rather a-historical article we had produced.

Prisoners can and do challenge, and sometimes change 're-strictions'. In fact E-Wing was at one time a crash course in the techniques required. Robinson once said to me after a diaspora of Spring 1968 that all the other Governors were getting onto him for exporting revolutionaries. That the facilities and controls are not now a great cause for complaint is a tribute to a small nucleus of determined and disruptive prisoners who were prepared to suffer for the privilege of challenging a highly restrictive and controlled régime. Applying crisis manipulation in an environment that was still administratively novel and untested, abetted by a newsmongering media, this régime was eroded in less than a year into the benign environment that you witnessed. Because there are no more arbitrary and capricious controls and because the demand for facilities is at the 'T.V. in the cell' stage the protest syndrome is an evolutionary hangover, but it is none the less there and can, if the circumstances are right, be effective. You saw it resurrected in a degenerate form in the megalomania of the antiphotograph campaign that burnt itself out on an issue that had a very real rationale to the enforcing agency, but the strength and endurance of the campaign was a measure of the successes that developed these techniques. Their real potency is in the no-man's-land of arbitrary interpretations; because they failed on a strategic issue and the conditions you witnessed never otherwise animated them, that is a far cry from saying they are powerless.

Not that everyday perception of the prison is typically influenced by such a grand vision; ideas of evolution, struggle and change are more likely to be evaluated at crisis points as they are during an arctic expedition or an epic mountain climb. For the most part the history of the wing is incorporated into more personal, more discrete anecdotes. Some of these are not specific to E-Wing. Many prisoners have stories to tell about the prison medical service, stories which prop up their belief in the cheap-jack nature of those organizations (aftercare, psychiatric, medical) which are supposedly set up to provide them with some form of service. These range from charges of cumulative neglect and indifference to a set of allegations about one Medical Officer killing a prisoner.

The stories which are told about riots, or M.O.s or Prison Officers are referred to as guides for action. But this does not mean that the men in E-Wing had an undifferentiated attitude towards authority. Their world was not just closed, but it was closed by certain identifiable figures. When we feel powerless and pushed around in the outside world, we attribute blame either to some vague constellation – 'them', the government, 'the way things are going' – or see a specific figure in each situation: we know it's the boss, the foreman, the teachers, our head of department. We can shift from the vague to the specific, from one figure to another and we are not always very clear about what each constellation of power really wants to do about us. In the prison, though the range of alternative figures is slight, few shifts are possible and it is all too clear what the immediately powerful are thinking.

In one sense all authority figures within prison are resented by inmates. They are all conceived of negatively by virtue of their position of authority. However, over and above this general hostility, there is a readiness to differentiate. Prisoners do distinguish good and bad prisons, good and bad Governors. Much of their discussion is spent upon the compilation of a demonology and hagiology of the prison world. We can best illustrate the range of qualifications which occur within the generally anti-authoritarian attitude by showing some pictures from the gallery. These pictures incorporate not merely contemporary attitudes, but also a shared historical interpretation of the way in which the men's lives have been controlled by others in the wing.

The Home Office

The Home Office is seen as conspiratorial and monolithic ('the judges and the Home Office planned it all together', 'Callaghan after all was head of the police before he became Home Secretary') but above all as capricious and arbitrary. Time and time again, the men note that the Home Office (this includes the Prison Department and other appendages) exert their power not with malice, but in a random, almost whimsical way. They are 'faceless bureaucrats', operating from behind a 'wall of silence' and it's never really clear why they make the decisions they do. As David writes, somewhat resignedly: 'My experiences over the years have convinced me of the existence of what Anthony Sampson calls the Home Office passion for unreform: the Home Office's particular brand of Catch-22-ism.'

This does not mean that the authority appears benign. The apparent capriciousness in the way in which men were transferred from one wing to another without any warning, was deeply resented. Jock wrote to us when one such series of moves was on the way: '. . . it's like Russian roulette here at the moment wondering who will disappear next.' Even if conditions improved in the wing there might still be an element of Catch-22, as Martin, one of the sex offenders isolated on a top landing, hinted in a conversation. He had said that he didn't mind moving to a larger wing, even if it meant giving up the physical facilities of E-Wing.

Stan: What sort of things are you thinking of?
Martin: Well, you know, things like that television set over there and the good food, being able to cook for ourselves and all that. It's quite comfortable here, we don't have any complaints about that. Actually, do you know what some people think when they see all these comforts? They think that they're just giving them to us because they're going to keep us here for ever. I don't think I feel like that myself, but that's what prisoners can think: that they're never going to be let out at all and that's why they're making it so comfortable.

This sort of double-bind perception ran through all the prisoners' dealings with bodies such as the Parole Board. They knew their own chances of parole to be very slender and gently mocked those who thought otherwise (one was described as 'praying to an effigy of Lord Hunt every morning') and there were frequent references to the somewhat bizarre relevance of the Parole Board Chairman's previous experience in the form of admonitions 'to be sure you were wearing your mountaineering boots when you appear before the Board'.[1] There is nothing in the history of the men's experience of the Home Office that invalidates their image and indeed much that confirms it. Jock, after long attempts to get permission for his common-law wife to visit him, was shown this reply from the Minister of State, Lord Stonham:

There is no general ban on visits by married women to men friends in prison, but the Secretary of State may under the Prison Rules impose restrictions upon communications between prisoners and others with a view to securing good order and discipline, or the prevention of crime and it was in the exercise of this power that Miss L—'s visits were disallowed. I have considered the matter once again, but I am unable to change the decision.

The men consider that this type of arbitrariness in Home Office correspondence arises from the isolation of civil servants. 'They have no idea what life inside is like.' We were certainly struck, when we visited officials at the Home Office, by the ironic similarity between their physical isolation and that of the prisoners over whom they kept surveillance. To meet the men who controlled the lives of top security prisoners we had to pass through a series of checks and counterchecks almost as stringent as those which controlled entrance to E-Wing.

1. At least Lord Hunt – as leader of the successful Everest expedition – was not unfamiliar with extreme environments.

Governors and Prison Officers

Here, perhaps more than with any other figures, judgements are highly personalized: good and bad governors along with good and bad nicks (a widely accepted maxim is that the Governor makes the prison) are firmly located in the gallery. In E-Wing Governors are particularly picked upon when examples of hypocrisy are required. There are several Governors who are noted for the way in which they maintain an urbane, soft façade but who are 'just the same old bastards underneath'.

The following are some of the most generally agreed judgements made during a single evening's discussion in which the class swapped comments on the various prisons and governors they had encountered:

Bad: 'Parkhurst is always so bad, that you can cut the atmosphere with a knife there;' 'At Parkhurst you don't walk down the stairs on your own because someone is bound to push you;' 'Mr B. actually stood there, watching the screws kicking blokes up, and he then went and joined in;' 'When I told Mr C. that the M.O. had nearly murdered a man he said that's none of your bloody business.'

Good: 'Maidstone is such a soft place, they wouldn't even know how to give a bloke a kicking there;' 'I always remember this time when the governor had to put some men on bread and water and actually went down to eat it with them.'

The men understood very well that authority at this level could afford to be liberal, putting the blame for anything unpleasant on the authoritarianism of the ordinary Prison Officer, the bureaucracy of the Home Office, and the pressures of political and public opinion. Governors, or more often Assistant Governors (with whom the men had closer contacts) were, as we have observed earlier, at least credited with some status and intelligence, attributes rarely allowed to the ordinary Durham Prison Officer.

In some prisons, screws may be accorded some qualified respect depending upon how well they meet prisoners' expectations. The Pentonville study suggests that screws are positively assessed according to their 'fairness, consistency, the degree to which the officer allows privileges and the decency with which he recognizes a prisoner's feelings'.[2] Negative attributes are 'the tendency to provoke, pettiness, victimization, untruthfulness and failure to keep promises'. However, in E-Wing, although some men make concessions of the 'they're just doing their job' type, there is a clear and unambiguous hostility to the screws. They are perceived as thick, insensitive, callous and above all – compared with the impersonal nature of Home Office control – spiteful, vindictive and personal. The type of screw who 'went for little things' was seen as epitomizing this group. The men have accumulated over their long years in the prison a substantial collective memory about the treatment they've received from Prison Officers and this memory cannot but influence their day-to-day behaviour. What this or that screw did is as relevant now as it was when he did it. One prisoner, Louis, told of how when he had been in solitary for a few days some years before, a screw went into his cell and tore up the photos of his children. He admitted that this incident coloured his everyday contemptuous treatment of all screws. They were people who did 'that sort of thing'.

This type of generalization is one way in which the prison world can be given a stable meaning. For many prisoners in E-Wing the existence of 'us' and 'them' was a starting point in their conception of prison life. From this followed attitudes to screws and M.O.s and governors. They may have recognized the existence of good screws, but this did not make any difference to their analysis. They told stories about good screws but in the end they were all bad, for they were on the wrong side. The presence of a good screw here or there was relatively unimportant and deserved no more attention than that which would be accorded by the conscientious Marxist to the

2. Terence and Pauline Morris, op. cit., pp. 264–5.

appearance of a philanthropist amongst the ranks of the ruling class. As the French anarchist Émile Henry remarked upon being castigated by a judge for endangering innocent people by bombing a cafe – 'There are *no* innocent bourgeois!'

Even when Prison Officers appear in novel contexts, wearing different uniforms and ostensibly performing different roles, they may still be negatively regarded. Tony Parker records the attitude of one prisoner to his new life in Grendon Underwood – Britain's much publicized first psychiatric prison.

The way you see these fellers talking to the screws, laughing and joking with them, they must be off their heads. A screw's a screw as far as I'm concerned: he always was and he always will be. There's one here, I spotted him the other day, I knew that man a few years back when I was in Wandsworth. They did a turnover of my cell, everything in it chucked about, the slop-bucket emptied all over the floor, the bedclothes thrown in the water, everything you can think of. And he was one of them that did it. Well, you can't tell me that man's changed; that now he's here he's going to be my friend and I'm going to be his, and all he wants in life is to help the prisoner. It's a good job I'm not on his wing, that's all I can say: the first chance I get I'll chin him, and I mean that.[3]

The men in E-Wing do not however live on a continual knife edge of aggression towards the screws; the situation does not allow this and they see little point in maintaining a complete façade of non-cooperation. They evolve an uneasy tolerance often combined with a sardonic distancing of themselves which takes the edge off any aggression.

The denigration of the guard is an important and often carefully worked out technique in itself. Beside generally putting the screws down in conversation, the men would set up incidents to confirm their stereotypes and also have some fun at the screws' expense. One game was to sit watching a television programme and at a pre-arranged signal, to suddenly burst out

3. Tony Parker, *The Frying Pan: A Prison and its Prisoners*, (London, Hutchinson, 1970), p. 153.

laughing. The prison officer on duty would come in to see what the joke on the programme was, at which point the men would relapse into serious attention.

Remarks were made such as: 'I remember there was a good screw at one place; he died! They came to me and said Mr Morgan has died and I had to try to look sad.' Then, on one occasion Paul recounted the (probably apocryphal) story of how there was a screw in one prison who just couldn't stand the job anymore and threw his keys on the ground and walked out. David's only comment on this was 'what a waste of all that training!'

There is then a relatively homogeneous set of attitudes to be found in E-Wing. There is not much ambiguity in the description of officers and Governors, there is generally agreement that the history of the wing was an evolutionary one in which the prisoners have slowly but surely gained some control over their environment. In what ways does this general agreement about the history of the wing and the nature of authority affect the level of solidarity in the wing?

Solidarity

There is some disagreement in studies of other prisons about the nature and extent of solidified inmate opposition to authority. Sykes and others consider that it should be quite clear to the prisoners that as they move towards greater solidarity, so they will be more effective in combatting the pains of imprisonment.[4] At the same time there are forces checking any such 'prisoner power': the guards, outnumbered and obsessed with control, try to keep the inmates divided, using the strong against the weak and playing on the inmate élite's vested interest in tranquillity. Other authors stress the origins of solidarity in the outside criminal culture: those institutions with a concentration of very experienced criminals also have the highest solidarity and anti-staff feeling.

4. Gresham Sykes. op. cit.

All these studies concede that the inmate code is often only shown verbal allegiance anyway and some observers are even more sceptical, suggesting that the prison is full of people who are unlikely to see any benefits from cooperation.[5] How does this relate to the E-Wing situation?

Firstly, there are many factors in E-Wing operating *against* solidarity. The security and control measures are so massive and pervasive that one would expect them to induce a profound sense of powerlessness among the prisoners. This fatalism might permeate all dealings with authority: the men's knowledge of their public reputation cannot but induce pessimism about their chances of fighting the Home Office, the Parole Board, the press. They have no illusions, either, of getting any sympathy if involved in a demonstration or disturbance.

Cohesion and solidarity also depend upon prolonged interaction between individuals. Restricted association of the type we have described works against this, and even more destructive of organization is the Prison Department's deliberate policy of transferring men around at regular intervals. The fact that such transfers are sudden and secret ensures their success in breaking up friendships and disturbing any cohesiveness or collective planning. Then, although the men obviously have much more in common than the motley collection of offenders found in most ordinary prisons, there are some critical differences between them. The differential between the sex offenders on the top floor, and the professionals on the bottom interferes with solidarity in the wing. We know of no collective action against authority which involved both these groups.

Finally – in comparison with the struggles inside some American prisons over the last few years – there are few common ideological ties among the E-Wing type of prisoner and certainly nothing like a common literature to provide collective motivations and justifications. The officers' traditional ability to destroy any potentially unified opposition by

5. Terence and Pauline Morris, *Pentonville: A Sociological Study of an English Prison*.

exploiting differences between the prisoners has been partially undermined in some American prisons by the rhetoric stressing political solidarity among inmates.[6] As was true of the older inmate code, this new rhetoric is not necessarily a description of what is actually happening – even in a handful of prisons. But it is clearly a powerful potential source of solidarity and one that is missing among British prisoners at this moment. The sources of the American prison movement rhetoric were ultimately derived from external political developments, and the absence of this rhetoric in prisons such as Durham attests not so much to the success of officials in insulating prisons and inmates, as to the fact that there is little to insulate them from. The Northern Ireland troubles, conflict over the immigration issue or industrial unrest could be seen as potential focus points for an inmate solidarity different from the one we detect, but we see no indication of any imminent change in this direction.

All this is counterbalanced by a group of factors which make for high loyalty and solidarity. The first arises from our delineation of the closed emotional world of the wing. Solidarity is partly inevitable because of the size of the group. It is too small for any important subgroups to be formed and for any such division to be exploited by authority; people are too physically close to each other all the time to let secrets out. Under such circumstances, there are few ways of avoiding solidarity.

6. The disturbances at Attica and elsewhere have differed from traditional prison riots in that the usual reformist ('housekeeping') demands – better food, medical care, visiting facilities, etc. – have been supplemented by more clearly political demands (civil and religious rights, protection from racism, the right to dissent) together with a rhetoric of collective bargaining and ideological confrontation. Organizations such as Prisoners Unions and, in a different way, the Black Panthers, have increased the solidarity of the 'convict class'. The few prison organizations in Britain such as Radical Alternatives to Prison (R.A.P.) which have attempted to move outside a conventional prison reform rhetoric have made little attempt to form a unified prisoners' movement, although the recent formation of P.R.O.P. may be a step in this direction.

No one can use the standard excuses for inactivity that are so important in non-prison life. 'I was somewhere else', 'I didn't know about it'. No one can even say 'I'll keep away because I'm due out soon.' Sartre has recalled the stress in his early work upon the necessity for man to make a decision: 'Whatever the circumstances, and wherever the site, a man is always free to choose to be a traitor or not.'[7] This he says was the simple problem during the resistance, a *for* or *against* which was a choice men could always make. Only later, says Sartre, did he realize this was too simple, that choices of political action in the contemporary world involved contradictions. The resistance situation, however, still applies in the security wing, although this does not mean that there are no acute personal dilemmas. One cannot remain uncommitted.

Another factor conducive towards solidarity is the 'nothing to lose' attitude. The argument raised in prison sociology about the ineffectiveness of most punishments within the prison is even more potent for long-term security men. There is very little the authorities can do: loss of a few weeks' or even months' remission is hardly a threat to men serving fifteen or twenty years. It was members of the Prison Officers' Association who were the first to complain about the natural life sentence passed upon the police killer Skingle in 1971. They recognized that the judge had placed within the prison system a man who had nothing to lose. And if loss of remission is hardly effective then solitary confinement and restricted diet is even less so. Men told us that a few days of solitary were often almost a welcome change from the type of emotional atmosphere we described earlier. In these circumstances risks can obviously be taken with some detachment.

A third factor making for solidarity is also connected with the prisoners' attitudes and value system. The gross power imbalance in the prison, coupled with the sheer monotony of a long sentence, encourages an ideology of risk taking which matches the criminal value system. To quote some comments

7. J.-P. Sartre quoted in an interview in *New Left Review*, March 1970.

made by two very different E-Wing prisoners, Roy and Chris:

Roy:

When the community largely consists of men with little hope for the future or the future exists only in terms of decades away, with no planned progression towards release, no tangible reinforcement or reward for behaviour allied to the fact that most of these men have been – in their eyes – rejected by society as a whole and a large percentage by their immediate families, wives, etc. is it not to be expected that bitterness will evidence itself in an anti-authoritarian form, owing no allegiance to the society who created it, and contains it, but only to the society of themselves – the loyalty of the prison culture – as exemplified at Parkhurst last year? . . . The creation of authority (the prison community) finally turns against it, in all probability with the knowledge that it cannot gain control but it can by its own action ensure a self-generating excitement, a sequence of events that at least prove that things – any form of 'things' – can happen, that life is not solely an authoritarian controlled existence of ennui, that one *can* break out of this, one can 'live' and not just exist, perhaps it entails living dangerously, perhaps leading finally to self-destruction but it does offer choice – the choice of existing the existence of non-events or living the life of events, good or bad, which are at least one's own creation.

In the following extract, Chris describes in more detail the ideology behind the 'dangerous living' referred to by Roy.

The lynchpin of this ideology is an ethic based on courage and the commitment to test it by risk taking in the quest for prestige and self-esteem, ranging from epitomizing gladiator virtues to challenging authority . . . The madness of all these institutions is that prisoners are allowed to operate on the same anti-social values that power crime outside. With no logical exploitation such as thieving or gangsterism available this largely revolves around the cult of toughness and prestigious rebel displays. The natural power struggle for social dominance that any group exhibits hots up in prison because the habitual outlets are blocked.

By drawing attention to the potency of such value systems, we are not suggesting that the prisoners are anything like agreed on the major issues that confront them. Their individual priorities may differ widely, as is illustrated clearly in the various struggles against visiting regulations.

For Jock, success or failure on this issue really mattered; someone he dearly wanted to see was being refused permission to visit. So, he could write in a letter with constant references to the 'wall of silence' and the 'faceless ones' in the Home Office:

I've no doubt it's some petty bureaucratic official occupying an office of sinecure suffering from some kind of mental disorder. He must be to deny visits to people in our kind of predicament. They really scrape the bottom of the barrel with the absurd and ludicrous reasons they come up with for denying visitors. I won't continue on this subject, as to me it's like I'm scratching an open wound.

Similarly, the issue of visiting was a personal priority for his brother Mike, whose wife had been heavily involved in outside agitation about the visiting regulations. During a visit while he was in Leicester, Mike's daughter had tried to go round the wooden bench that separated them to sit on his lap. An officer tried to stop her and Mike lashed out at him. For this he was punished under Rule 43 and lost six months' remission. Justifiably he was bitter about the whole issue and constantly exposed himself to punishment for not accepting the regulations.

Paul, Louis and David, on the other hand, had very few outside contacts anyway and although they fought with considerable persistence, one felt that the issue itself was less important than the collective need to make some gesture. This 'distance' was indicated in a letter received from David after a prolonged hunger strike about the visiting regulations:

No doubt you've read that our morbid desire for publicity led us to refuse to eat. Well, we're all eating again and the wing is back to normal. We don't appear to have influenced anybody, but then I didn't think we would. I would not recommend a fourteen day fast to anyone.

Such differences in the intensity of commitment matter much less when the possibilities of collective action arise. Then, solidarity is essential: the part the individual plays becomes immediately salient to everyone and is eventually a way of defining his position in the wing's private history.

Observers of other extreme situations invariably record how the demands made at crisis points, when things are going wrong, somehow 'bring out the best and worst' in people or 'show who your real friends are'. In prisons, any collective action, such as participation in a riot, can provide the opportunity for such redefinitions. As one riot participant recalls: 'During that forty-eight hour period the hand of the clock stopped, and incidents – some funny, others tragic – became superimposed on a background of timelessness. In some instances casual acquaintances become close friends, and in others, men who had previously been close friends, became dreaded enemies.'[8]

Expeditions arrive at their destination and are dissolved, short termers leave the prison and don't have to continue living with the friends and enemies made during a riot. But for long term prisoners, the redefinitions remain and have to be lived with. Such knowledge raised acute dilemmas for some of the prisoners. As Roy wrote, about a painful decision on whether or not to participate in a hunger strike:

Can own choice prevail against community's tenets and still remain in good standing? Or does one opt out of community life and become a solitary, an outsider, owing neither allegiance to community or authority . . . I cannot walk the dividing line, it's impossible. By 'vice' of sentence I 'belong' to the prison community yet have great difficulty at times in identification . . .

Ultimately, whether or not men felt full sympathy with other inmate's aims, solidarity would usually prevail. Lessons which have been learned in the history of the wing are principally responsible for this. United demands have worked and

8. H. Jack Griswold et. al. *An Eye For An Eye*, (New York, Pocket Books, 1971), p. 152.

have been shown to work in the past. There have been small, but significant individual victories such as those of the 'stew episode': the men refused to continue eating the daily stew and threatened a mass hunger strike if the diet was not varied. This worked almost immediately. Then there have been the cumulative successes of the campaigns and riots to which we refer elsewhere.

All this does not mean that there is a continual state of rebellion. The day-to-day life of the prison – as in the case of most societies – is marked by tranquillity and resignation. However, the potential for solidarity is there and it lies at the back of many of the individual and collective forms of fighting back we now proceed to describe.

CHAPTER SIX

Making out and fighting back

'I'll keep on trying to escape for another seven years.
If I can't get out by then I'll settle down.'
Louis

In Christopher Burney's account of his internment in occupied
France, he recalls that soon after arriving in prison he heard a
great noise from an opposite part of the building. 'It was only
. . . later that I learned that the prisoners in the other building
were in those days common-law criminals, with nothing re-
spectably resistant about them, but I admired their spirits and
envied their adaptability.'[1] So he begrudgingly admires them,
although as ordinary criminals rather than political prisoners
their resistance was not really respectable. The political prisoner
(the spy, the prisoner of war) is allowed to fight back against
his captors. He must actively resist torture (even die rather
than give away secrets), try to escape, join with his fellows in
making life as difficult as possible for the authorities. The
noble nature of such battles is enshrined in those innumerable
British prisoner of war films where the heroes – everyone
British – seem to spend all their time planning escapes, digging
tunnels, making fun of their loutish captors and generally being
a nuisance.

All this is just a variant of the general romantic vision of
extreme situations in which the man who fights back, who
overcomes his environment, who refuses to be beaten down,
whatever the odds, is the hero. In fact the defining characteristic of this vision is the presence of such a hero. Generations
of children have been brought up on adventure stories set on

1. Christopher Burney, *Solitary Confinement*, p. 36.

battlefields, oceans, mountains, jungles, deserts and ice-caps where the essential theme is man's struggle against the environment. The theme is repeated in the low to middle brow adult equivalents of these stories (the novels of Alistair MacLean, magazines such as *Man*, *Adventure*, *Real Man*) and finds its intellectual echoes in the heroic literature of Hemingway, Conrad and Melville.

In this latter representation – and perhaps implicitly throughout the tradition – the hero does much more than struggle against inexorable odds to survive. He must do more than just keep alive. He proves or even increases his humanity by rendering harmless both man-made horrors (prisons, torture, labour camps, enforced deprivation) and natural hazards (jungles, killer whales, snowstorms). Indeed, sometimes, he actively seeks such horrors out – like Mailer's Steve Rojack (in *An American Dream*) who submits himself to the terrors of walking on the thin ledge of a tower block and Conrad's Kurtz who goes further into the Heart of Darkness.

But under certain circumstances, those who fight back under similar conditions, are not endowed with the same heroic nature. Indeed, like Christopher Burney, one is even surprised that this sort of person would have the nerve to resist at all. The long-term prisoner who fights back is not endowed with personal qualities such as nerve, bravery and 'character' nor is he allowed anything like an acceptable set of motives – let alone an ideology – through which his behaviour could be comprehended. When he tries to escape, goes on a hunger strike, makes a nuisance of himself by composing letters and petitions, smuggles information out or refuses to accept the rules of the system, he is a 'troublemaker' who 'can't take his medicine'. There are of course exceptions to this – especially in the daring escape which strikes a note of romantic admiration in the public – but on the whole the criminal who can't take his punishment is condemned.

Making out in Institutions

Sociologists who have studied prisons have at least been prepared to consider resistance more as a type of reaction to prison conditions than as evidence for the existence of pathological traits in inmates. Nevertheless, the starting point for most such studies is a concern about the relative absence of organized resistance within prison, about the degree of order, the general lack of riots and outbreaks. These approaches concentrate upon the prison as a system which by and large maintains itself in a state of equilibrium, a state which depends upon a complex set of checks and balances. The inmates are not involved in continual resistance; the system, which cannot maintain itself by resorting to brute force or by calls upon the men's loyalty, buys them off with a number of concessions.[2] In addition groups of inmates, through the corruption of prison officers, also come to exert a force for order. Power which is gained by them is exerted against their fellow men in the interests of the status quo, rather than against the authorities. The authorities in turn, recognize the realities of the situation and operate the prison not just through the official personnel but also through the clique of powerful inmates. No one wants to rock the boat. The typical reaction of the prisoner to his predicament is therefore dulled acceptance.

Goffman's inmates are also seen as fundamentally passive members of their institutions.[3] Their fight is primarily about the nature of the identity that the institution is trying to impose on them. Given that the fight is defined in these terms, and that the institution from which Goffman's main evidence is derived is a mental hospital, it is not surprising that the struggle is not of a very disruptive kind, and is viewed in individual rather than collective terms. Thus, while Goffman concedes that inmate organization in prisons has sometimes been strong

2. For the full argument about the 'defects of total power' in prisons, see Gresham Sykes, *The Society of Captives: A Study of a Maximum Security Prison*.

3. Erving Goffman, *Asylums*.

enough to run strikes and short-lived insurrections and that strong underground organizations have developed in prisoner-of-war and even concentration camps, he sees such concerted action as the exception rather than the rule. His point is that inmates tend to *adapt* rather than actively *resist*.

He therefore concentrates on the personal lines of adaptation the inmate might employ at different phases of his moral career. These different 'tacks' are: situational withdrawal, in which the inmate withdraws from all but immediate bodily involvements; the intransigent line in which 'the inmate intentionally challenges the institution by flagrantly refusing to cooperate with staff'; colonization: 'the sampling of the outside world provided by the establishment is taken by the inmate as the whole, and a stable relatively contented existence is built up out of the maximum satisfaction procurable within the institution' and finally, conversion: 'the inmate appears to take over the official or staff view of himself and tries to act out the role of the perfect inmate'.

The only really active resistance role that Goffman allows for is the intransigent line and even this only involves a refusal to cooperate and further it is 'typically a temporary and initial phase of reaction, with the inmate shifting to situational withdrawal or some other line of adaptation'. These modes of adaptation are essentially tension-reducing in their functions: 'Each tack represents a way of managing the tension between the home world and the institutional world.'

Fighting Back

It is difficult to relate these 'adaptive' accounts to the contemporary American situation, where in some prisons general adjustment to the system has long since given way to a continuous coordinated active resistance, or with our own findings which indicated a high level of resistance amongst the men at Durham. When the prisoners there chose to go along with the system, they did so as a way of overcoming certain local problems rather than as a method for dealing with the general problem of surviving. This emphasis upon resistance may have been made easier in E-Wing by the absence of a power élite with a 'vested interest in tranquillity'. It was undoubtedly advanced by the fact that the prisoners had little to bargain for in return for accommodating to the system. Privileges were rarely given, or in the context of the length of the sentences were virtually meaningless. Security regulations meant that continuous daily checks were made of men's possessions, and embryonic groups were readily broken by the regular and sudden transfers of prisoners from one security wing to another.

A further factor which increased the likelihood of resistance amongst the prisoners in E-Wing and which differentiated them from some other institutionalized groups was the relatively minor impact of the 'degradation' ceremonies upon the men's sense of identity. Such ceremonies (exchanging one's name for a number, adoption of prison clothes, loss of personal possessions) were already familiar to most of the men and had long since ceased to be fundamentally disconcerting. Most of the maximum security prisoners had developed through their criminal career a sense of personal identity which readily insulated them from the attacks upon their self images launched by judges, psychiatrists and prison governors.

Our reservations about the standard sociological accounts of adaptation to institutional life can be summarized thus:

i) the inmate is portrayed as an essentially passive creature whose adaptations – ingenious as they sometimes might be – are somewhat pathetic in nature. He cannot fight, he can only learn how to accept in a more comfortable way.

ii) the depiction of subcultures, underlife, and secondary adjustments tells us little about the meaning of such phenomena to the group concerned, and the way they can be used, manipulated or exploited in diverse ways.

iii) the similarities of the inmates' resistance to ordinary political resistance are played down because they are not accredited with an ideology which could legitimate such fighting back (e.g. to save their country, to uphold their sense of dignity and honour etc.).

iv) Almost all accounts in prison sociology of what it was like and what struggles and accommodations took place between the inmates and the authorities are non-historical in character. That is, the unique nature of the setting, the prison's history beyond the one or two years of the research, is ignored.

Types of Resistance

We will now distinguish five types of resistance used in the wing. Variants of these appear in other prison literature which is not just concerned with long-term imprisonment, but we believe that it is only in extreme situations that these types emerge with particular clarity, contrasted as they are in the men's perception with the alternative of retreating from life for the next ten to twenty years. The types of resistance are not mutually exclusive. Different ones may be adapted by the same prisoner at different times, and neither are they clearly linked to a particular period of the prisoner's sentence. We will nevertheless maintain in the next chapter that the adoption or persistence of certain ideologies is linked to the favoured type of resistance. The types are: self-protecting; campaigning; escaping; striking; and confronting.

1. Self-Protecting

This type ranges from the habitual attempts to make life more bearable in the prison – Goffman's secondary adjustments – to active or passive individual refusal to cooperate with the staff (intransigence) and a deliberate challenging of staff rules.

The existence of secondary adjustments – all the ingenious devices for getting more and better food, varying the daily routine, improving one's cell and building up some privacy – can be taken for granted. We do not want to spend much time describing what we agree are – in Clemmer's term – universal features of prisonization. They are not especial preoccupations of the E-Wing men.

More important here, are the ways in which the inmate beats off the unfavourable definitions offered to him. No single monolithic set of definitions was presented to the prisoners by all those they encountered, they were all aware though of three dominant ways in which others labelled them. The one revolves around their pariah status as the most vicious, depraved, thuggish, evil men in the prisons; the other (given wide credence by prison officers and some journalists) concerns their supposedly privileged position as members of the pampered élite whose sentences are softened by the 'easy' life in the security wings; the final one concerns their symbolic representation (particularly by the judges who sentenced them) as persons who are 'repaying a debt to society' or from whom 'society deserves a rest' (to quote the judge's remarks at the end of the Kray case). None of these labels offer exactly dignified and acceptable self conceptions.

Their response to these labels ranges from partial acceptance (for example, of their élite role), through amused detachment (we would receive Christmas cards signed 'Rent-A-Thug' and frequent reassurances that if our professors were giving us trouble we should let them know we had friends in the underworld) to total and bitter rejection.

This type of humorous evasion of popular definitions contrasts with much of the literature on total institutions which presents the inmate as someone who has been stripped of all other identifications and is forced to play the single all-embracing inmate role twenty-four hours a day. He is said to desperately resort to protective and assertive devices in order to claim that he is someone other than a convict or a patient. While this picture is not implausible, there are two important processes at work in E-Wing which undermine its comprehensiveness. In the first place, it is not true that the prisoner receives no recognition of himself in any other role – in correspondence with relatives and friends, in contacts with us, in newspaper reports and even books about the better known of them, the men are constantly being reminded of other identities. They may receive letters from outsiders who take an interest in them as persons, reminding them of previous good times and old friends; they correspond with people who might regard them as experts (one of the men told us how he had 'mildly rebuked' his M.P. for voting the wrong way in the abolition debate). Sometimes these outside identities can be embarrassing and they try to distance themselves from such roles: one of the men, who was always trying – with justification – to deny involvement in violence, was, to his annoyance, referred to by the others as 'The Cosher'. Secondly, the men seem to have transcended the use of desperate regulative devices to overcome role-stripping. They would not agree to a statement such as that made by one Pentonville prisoner:

. . . you need to put on a front in prison . . . hide one's feelings and thoughts behind a cheerful expression and a smile. In prison one must behave and act like a con at all times, even if this is different from the way one would behave and act outside.[4]

The E-Wing prisoners simply do not hide their feelings and thoughts (if anything, the opposite is true and there is very little pretence) nor do they play the role of the con at all times. They often identify themselves – for example along dimensions of political beliefs – in terms which have little to do with the convict role.

It is not just a question of the use of conscious ploys to distance themselves from this role. As we remarked in regard to the saliency of their criminal records, there are many situations in which they *can* be other than what they are supposed to be. The following is an illustration of non-self-conscious expression of normality:

In the course of a discussion on violence in the mass media, one of us read out a passage from a cheap sex/gangster story. After a few lurid sentences about groins being kicked, grunts

4. Terence and Pauline Morris, *Pentonville: A Sociological Study of an English Prison*, p. 117.

of agony, and blood spilling, one of the men remarked: 'That sort of thing doesn't do a thing to me. I don't know how anyone could say it could cause people to go out and be violent.' Another of the men interrupted: 'Yes, Dave, but you're a normal person. I mean just imagine what it might do to someone who can't control himself.' At this point the whole class laughed self-consciously – the 'normal' man the remarks had been addressed to was in prison for a double murder. Not only was his normality taken for granted, but, in the context, it was perfectly justified: one simply could not imagine David being affected by such writing.

Here though, we are concerned with the tactics which are conscious. How does one retain a sense of value and importance in a hostile environment which is loaded with problems and which presents so undignified a set of definitions of self to serve as props?

The first protective device is self-consciousness itself. Right through the literature on extreme situations – from polar expeditions to labour camps – one finds a reiteration of the need to make sense of one's experience. Bettelheim records how at the beginnng of his period in a concentration camp he started asking himself whether he was going insane: he noticed disturbing changes in previously 'normal' prisoners.[5] At this point, in order to protect himself from becoming as they were, he embarked on his inquiry into what was happening to himself and others. This was the form of self-defence that Hilde Bluhm found in every one of the twelve autobiographical accounts by concentration camp survivors which she examined:[6]

. . . the ego of the prisoners refused to accept the estrangement it was subjected to. It therefore turned the experiences connected with the loss of its feelings into an object of its intellectual interests.

5. Bruno Bettelheim, *The Informed Heart*.
6. Hilde O. Bluhm, 'How Did They Survive? Mechanisms of Defense in Nazi Concentration Camps', *American Journal of Psychology*, 2 (1948), pp. 3–32.

She goes on to note that although self-expression, through hobbies, or study and writing about outside matters also helped, this was too remote:

> Those ... who embarked on a study of the concentration camp proper, turned towards that very reality which had threatened to overpower them; and they rendered that reality into an object of their 'creation'. This turn from a passive suffering to an active undertaking indicated that the ego was regaining control.

We stress this point not just because of its importance in trying to understand how people cope with extreme situations, but because its repeated affirmation by survivors suggests the first rule for any handbook on survival: *understand what is happening to you.* Thus, as Bluhm concludes about the camps: 'the association between self-observation and self-expression became a most successful means of survival.' Or, as Genet expresses it more simply in his introduction to George Jackson's prison letters: 'In prison more than elsewhere one cannot afford to be casual.' [7]

The E-Wing men see this and they were anything but casual in the way they handled problems of time, the fears of deterioration, the complexities of their interrelationships. But self-observation is not always easy for them and is not encouraged by the authorities who seem to retain some cultural belief that too much brooding (rather like too much masturbation) can be a bad thing. Thus one well-known prisoner was not even allowed to read an objectionable and tendentious biography of himself. As one prison official opposed to this prohibition remarked: 'If he can't read about his own life, who can?' One is also reminded again of the bizarre set of regulations which technically prevent a prisoner writing about himself or prison conditions.

An allied form of protection is mind-building. A favourite occupation in prisons is body-building, which besides its overt

7. George Jackson, *Soledad Brother: The Prison Letters of George Jackson*, (Penguin, 1971).

function in keeping one fit and strong, also allows flouting one's strength in front of the guards. (One of the particularly strong prisoners we knew used to occasionally threaten the screws with the weights he was lifting.) But just as important for the men we knew, was the ability to flaunt themselves symbolically with increased knowledge from classes and private reading. We have referred already to the delight the men obtained at a screw's satisfaction on being told that he was an 'aggressive psychopath'. Labels such as 'lumpen' were used with similar enjoyment. David is a typical mind-builder. He never tried to escape although he had been in the wing during several escape attempts. His struggle is intellectual. He read Plato at night, and then forced his mates to walk up and down with him in the morning while he told them about it. He knows he bores them – but he also knows that it keeps him going. He is not a solitary reader, nor an obsessive collector of knowledge, but rather someone who uses study to socially assert himself. He is delighted when he can score off a screw or off other inmates by using his learning. His style of confrontation with the social world around him is similar to that adopted by the more traditional rebels – the escapers and the prison militants; the self is realized against the institution rather than within it. Goffman described the paradox inherent in this type of self-realization:

Without something to belong to, we have no stable self, and yet total commitment and attachment to any social unit implies a kind of selflessness. Our sense of being a person can come from being drawn into a wider social unit; our sense of selfhood can arise through the little ways in which we resist the pull. Our status is backed by the solid buildings of the world, while our sense of personal identity often resides in the cracks.[8]

Such mind-building and pre-occupation with intellectual or artistic interest is seen in the psychoanalytically influenced literature on extreme situations (such as concentration camps) as a form of sublimation: Kautsky records 'there was no better

8. Erving Goffman, *Asylums*, p. 320.

means against hunger than discussions on Goethe or Mozart, on mountain climbing and swimming, on beautiful Paris or Geneva...'[9] Such extreme physical deprivations did not obtain in E-Wing, and in any event we think that mind-building serves a broader purpose than sublimation. It is close to what Irwin calls 'gleaning': the way in which convicts choose to radically change their life styles and follow a carefully devised plan to 'better themselves', 'improve their mind' or 'find themselves' while in prison.[10] In an even broader sense, such attempts are connected – as we will discuss in the next chapter – with quests for legitimate deviant identities such as 'intellectual outsider', 'bohemian', or 'exile'.

2. Campaigning

In all prisons there is a mode of fighting back which involves formalizing such responses as moaning, niggling, complaining and making a nuisance of oneself. The prisoner leaks stories to the press, continually raises issues with such bodies as the Visiting Magistrates Committee, organizes petitions and writes letters to his M.P. and agencies such as the National Council for Civil Liberties, N.A.C.R.O., R.A.P., Justice, European Commission on Human Rights. Although all long-term prisoners are involved to some degree in this activity, there are some who pursue it with such dedication and persistence that they become regarded by the staff and other prisoners as professional campaigners and this virtually becomes a style of doing one's time.

Such attempts to impove conditions and overcome deprivations are allied to what Thomas Mathiesen, in his study of a medium security prison in Norway called censoriousness.[11] This term covers the ways in which the inmate, rather than fighting the established norms, uses them against authority

9. Kautsky, quoted in Bluhm, op. cit., p. 28.
10. John Irwin, *The Felon*, (New Jersey, Prentice Hall, 1970).
11. Thomas Mathiesen, *The Defences of the Weak*, (London, Tavistock, 1965).

figures. He points a finger at them and accuses them of being unjust and unfair by their own rules. In E-Wing censoriousness is not – as Mathiesen found – an alternative to peer group solidarity, but goes along with such solidarity. Right from the first days of the wing there have been numerous campaigns and petitions; in very few of which, as far as we know, did anyone break ranks. In 1965 two separate petitions alleging ill-treatment were smuggled out of the wing and one prisoner obtained wide publicity from a complaint to the Commission on Human Rights about lights being on in the cells all night, the lack of association and the size of the exercise yard (then fifteen by ten feet). The most notable of later examples was the long sustained campaigns (which we have referred to quite often) about the visiting regulations.

The personal record for campaigning is probably held by Robert. A summary of his letters and petitions over the last decade of imprisonment is given overleaf. It is important to note in view of the comments we made in Chapter Three that the mere writing of these letters is no evidence of their eventual delivery.

There is a peculiarly ironic side to this example of campaigning in that our conversations with the authorities suggest that they, like Robert, recognize the value of such an enterprise for the prisoner's adaptation to his long sentence. They think that it keeps him going! But this is a vicious circle, in that such views then allow them to write off his petitions and letters as the work of an amiable crank. We have read a great deal of this correspondence in conjunction with the replies from the authorities and consider that Robert's letters, far from showing evidence of obsessiveness or crankiness, constitute an exceptionally effective indictment of the hypocrisies which underlie contemporary penal practice in this country. For example, he repeatedly draws attention to the 'Catch-22' situation in which he is required to show evidence of retraining as a qualification for parole whilst as a Category 'A' prisoner, being officially denied any opportunities for such retraining.

Campaigns are of two kinds: those directing attention to

individual grievances (usually about the prisoners' original conviction) and those referring to collective complaints about prison conditions. The first kind has never had much chance of success while the second has – in E-Wing at least – had a cumulative success in changing conditions for the better over the years. The men's constant niggling and vigilance has paid off – although it is difficult to separate this effect from the more dramatic results of investigations and changes forced on the authorities by the type of confrontations we describe later in this chapter.

On the whole, though, campaigns are principally calculated to annoy; there is little feeling that one will get anywhere. This

Letters to M.P.s	130
Letters to Lord Soper	7
Lord Longford	67
Lady Wootton	44
National Council for Civil Liberties	23
Solicitor	113
Quakers	24
Lord Chancellor	3
Amnesty	5
UNA Commission on Human Rights	5
Merfyn Turner	49
Lord Hunt	5
New Law Journal	2
National Association for Care and Resettlement of Offenders	7
Law Society	3
Parole Board	9
Various Organizations	18
Other Individuals	28
	545

In addition he sent 63 petitions to the Home Office

is particularly true of campaigns directed at the Home Office. The men argue that there is no rational pattern to Home Office decisions, so why should they waste time in trying to present a rational case? At most one can hope that the continual bombardment will annoy some harassed bureaucrat who might eventually reverse a decision on grounds as unpredictable and whimsical as those which led him to defend it in the first place.

3. Escaping

Self-protecting and campaigning are distinguished from other forms of fighting back in that they are essentially individual in character. Although many of the techniques of self-defence that we described are learned through the group, it is more or less up to the individual to decide whether or not to employ them. And while campaigning is obviously helped by support from one's fellows, this support is not absolutely necessary. The questions of loyalty and solidarity we described earlier are not of paramount importance, whereas escapes from a small security wing obviously require some form of collaboration, if only the passive collaboration of keeping quiet about the preparations. All the men knew at least three weeks in advance of the plan for the MacVicar/Probyn escape from E-Wing. The fact that the escape did not go through as intended was due to another prisoner in the main part of the prison sounding the alarm. Despite such spectacular escapes – and others in the last few years such as those of Biggs and Blake – most of the prisoners did not see escape as a realistic possibility. Thinking about it could be pleasant and disconcerting and it obviously served an important function in relationship to authority, whose main and sometimes sole role, was seen in terms of preventing escapes. Indeed, one well-liked Assistant Governor used to ritualistically tell new arrivals to the wing: 'Your job is to try to escape, mine is to prevent you from escaping.' Escape attempts are in this sense a form of concurring with the official system's view of the inmate.

This almost ritualistic element in the relationship was

indicated in one of the prisoner's reply to the Assistant Governor's line: 'I'll keep on trying to escape for another seven years. If I can't get out by then I'll settle down.'

4. Striking

One of the most accepted weapons of non-violent resistance in political and religious conflict, has been the hunger strike. It is especially useful in a prison, where it would be meaningless to withdraw from any other commitment, least of all that of performing one's daily work. Industrial striking has no meaning in this context. However, the threat of a hunger strike until death from a person who is serving a life sentence, despite having a particular irony which is not lost on prisoners or staff, is likely to prompt some humanitarian response. There were several collective hunger strikes in the wing – primarily over the visiting regulations – but striking is still an important weapon for the individual who doesn't want to involve others in his protest or whose grievance is wholly private.

For this reason the several major hunger strikes in the wing have taken place on the 'fours', the upper landing in which the isolated sex criminals were segregated. This form of resistance was used most persistently by Frank in his long and as yet unsuccessful campaign to be allowed to see a particular visitor. In the space of one year, he went on three hunger strikes, the first lasting thirty days, the second fifty and the third seventy-one. In each case he was moved to the prison hospital early on during the strike and eventually tube fed. We know too little about the dynamics of this form of resistance to speculate on what functions other than the narrowly political ones it served. It is worth noting that in Frank's case particularly the strikes were invariably accompanied by salacious attention from the mass media, often with the implicit criticism of the prison authorities for going to so much trouble in keeping such men alive.

5. Confronting

Prisoners' rights have become a major concern of radicals in the United States in recent years. This is not because sensitive revolutionaries have decided to turn to the problem of imprisonment but because direct confrontationist tactics by inmates have forced the problem into public consciousness. The prison has always been a popular metaphor for society, but now it has gained a special political value. The fact that most prisoners are black at a time when blackness is becoming increasingly synonymous with revolutionary intention helps to transform large numbers of criminals, who were previously mere thieves and murderers, into political prisoners. When Bob Dylan mourns the death of George Jackson he observes that in this world all of us are either prisoners or guards and thereby confirms the popular radical feeling that the most vivid contemporary way to describe class and racial conflict is by resorting to a prison metaphor.

The development of this type of perspective pushes the prisoner into an ideological position which entails confrontation with authority. The other styles of fighting back we have described are less appropriate. One does not try to gain small victories over the guards for in the very attempt one may in some small way acknowledge the legitimacy of their position. Campaigning is particularly alien to this ideological perspective for it implies more than any other style of adaptation that the authorities can be reasoned with, that they can be made to see the error of their ways. Similarly escape, unless it involves a mass outbreak, may be regarded as ideologically unsound in so far as its individualistic adventurous nature conflicts with the norm of collective solidarity which characterizes revolutionary groups.

Direct confrontation becomes then the most appropriate style of fighting back for those groups who can unite under an anti-authoritarian ideological banner, and who can manifest sufficient solidarity to counteract the inevitably harsh retaliation by the authorities. Two major cases of confrontation have occurred at Durham and have been described elsewhere in some detail. The anti-authoritarianism of these mutinees derived much more from the inmates' attitudes described in the last chapter rather than from an articulated revolutionary ideology. They were therefore hardly English Atticas, but they certainly demanded a high degree of solidarity and a readiness to take chances in a relatively powerless situation. The localized nature of these disturbances, their irregular appearance, and their sudden conclusion suggest that they depend more upon the insensitivity of the authorities than upon any growing political consciousness amongst the inmates.

With all the talk of mutiny, rebellion and insurrection which surrounded these events, it might still be tempting to see such resistance as political in character. In these and other conflicts the analogy with the industrial situation is all too readily made. The rhetoric is of negotiation, mediation, talks breaking down and settlements. In the parley before a disturbance in 1968 the Assistant Governor asked an inmate leader: 'How long is it going to be this time?' to which the reply was: 'About fourteen days I should think.' It is tempting, but we believe mistaken, to read too much into such analogies. Not only do these prisoners not behave like this most of the time, nor authority see the situation in this way, but the balance of power is more totally on one side than is ever the case on the factory floor.

Only amongst the small black group in our Eccleston sample have we found any indication of a collective political sentiment, and even here the questionnaire which was used revealed little more than a simple feeling that the length of their sentences represented racial prejudice in their judges. Unless prison authorities manifest particular insensitivity during the coming years, we would not expect direct confrontation to be a popular form of fighting back. When it does occur, however, its impact upon the consciousness of those involved is considerable. While it may rely for its appearance upon the presence of a crude anti-authoritarian ideology, it certainly leaves behind it a sense of common identity and purpose which helps even more than the activity itself to keep away the pains of imprisonment.

CHAPTER SEVEN

Identities, biographies and ideologies

'Prison is an experimental laboratory for all the
emotional and social problems. It's so clear-cut here.
So diagrammatic. So easy to observe the forces that
wrench us apart and bring us together. It's been a
revelatory event.'

Timothy Leary

We have not talked very much about the actual men in E-Wing.
We have described their problems, common attitudes and styles
of fighting back but we have hardly referred at all to the
inmates' self-identities; nor discussed them as *persons* with
distinctive backgrounds and ideas. In this chapter we want to
stress their diversity of personality and life styles, the heterogeneity of their approaches to life and crime and prison. If we
had omitted this type of discussion we would have been in
good company, for many of the best-known studies of institutions have confined themselves to treating the inmates as a
group who could be understood almost entirely in terms of their
common experiences as members of an institution. The basis
for this view lies in the idea of institutions as 'people-proces-
sing' factories. Goffman and others are so impressed with the
degree of mortification of the self which is said to occur at the
moment of entry to an institution that they tend to assume
the pre-institutional self loses its importance, that a new institutional identity is created which has more claims upon our
attention.

In other non-sociological studies of the effects of extreme
environments, we find that great attention is paid to the personal characteristics of those who expose themselves to such extreme conditions. In everyday evaluations of extreme situations
we recognize very clearly that the same conditions will mean

different things to different men and will therefore produce very different reactions. We say of the lone round-the-world yachtsman 'only a nut like him could have survived' and, if we are interested in such exploits, we look for explanations of their success or failure in terms of the adventurer's biography, attitudes to life, family relationships, etc. One recent student of great individual exploits in exploration and adventure finds in their heroes a common 'Ulysses factor' which includes properties such as courage, selfishness, physical strength, ability to lead, self-discipline, endurance, cunning, unscrupulousness and even strong sexual attraction.[1] Such dimensions are also explicitly recognized in the way in which people are carefully selected for hazardous exploits. The army officer who hand picks the unit that is to operate in the jungle for indefinite periods, decides which men have the appropriate character for such an experience. The battery of psychological tests used to screen men for long duties in submarines, polar expeditions or space travel, is just a more sophisticated application of this principle. But, however commonly this principle is applied, it is by no means clear whether personal biographies are more or less important in predicting behaviour in extreme situations than they are in everyday routines of life.

We have asserted that the men in E-Wing hardly lost their identities as a result of being processed through the prison system. Being processed did not seem to have significantly changed them. They frequently joked about the labels which others had attempted to fix upon them, they asserted their superiority over their guards, and developed ways of dealing with attacks upon their self conceptions. The inmate culture of E-Wing cannot be fully understood if we regard it as a simple product of life in the wing. It is not just the history of the wing that is important to the inmate culture; we must also take account of the history of the men who make up its population.

1. J. R. L. Anderson, *The Ulysses Factor*, (London, Hodder & Stoughton, 1970).

John Irwin and Donald Cressey reached a similar conclusion in their prison research and were forced to differentiate the prison culture into a 'criminal code' and an 'inmate code'.[2] The criminal code, or the 'thief subculture', was not a product of prison life. It emphasized the importance of getting out quickly. It stressed that one was a man rather than a prisoner, and that one must do one's own time and not interfere with others. Prison was to be regarded as an annoying interval in one's career. Men who subscribed to this code were inclined to be snobs within the prison, they 'kept themselves to themselves' but they would engage in mutual aid when they felt that another prisoner required help. This code contrasted with the 'inmate code' in which utilitarianism reigned. Members who subscribed to this latter ideology chased after scarce resources in the prison, they attempted to capitalize upon inside chances of acquiring status and they placed a price upon help as much as they did upon any of the other goods they hoarded for distribution. Their life was lived within the prison.

This argument at least allows the biographies of the prisoners a place in prison life; it increases the permeability of the membrane between prison and external society. But its resort to the concept of 'thief subculture' to characterize the external inputs to the prison system is not subtle enough to catch the range of identities (for example, religious or political) which can be brought into the prison from the outside world.

Category A prisoners might appear at first to be a homogenous group who share a similar criminal code: certainly the mass media refer to them as 'the most dangerous men behind bars', as 'super-criminals' and the Radzinowicz Report lumps them together as 'young, or fairly young, violent professional criminals who are both dangerous and persistent in their criminal activities'. But speaking with a calculated restraint, we would say that the men we met during our three years of research displayed a greater number of distinctive life styles,

2. John Irwin and Donald Cressey, 'Thieves, Convicts and the Inmate Culture', *Social Problems*, (Autumn 1962, pp. 142–55).

a wider spectrum of opinions and ideologies than have been present in any other group we have ever encountered.

Criminal Careers and Prison Adaptations

In the first place distinctions need to be made in terms of the criminal careers which led to the men's imprisonment. In the wing we met men who had been persistently involved in a variety of illegal and semi-legal business schemes; there were those who had helped to organize protection rackets, and others who had persistently engaged in deviant sexual behaviour or who had resorted to armed robbery. There were men who had organized a series of complex thefts and men who had suddenly and unexpectedly murdered. There were persistent escapers, whose criminal career involved conventional larceny, and political prisoners who had made a career of passing on secrets.

The men differed not only in their actual crimes but also in their commitments to a criminal career. There were those whose involvement in crime had lasted years and those for whom it had lasted minutes. Some of the men had enjoyed considerable publicity during their careers while others had operated in conditions of maximum secrecy. Some had been involved with large groups of fellow criminals; others had operated entirely alone.

It is true that the majority of these men had used violence at one time or another. It was this after all, more than any other aspect of their lives, which had brought them to E-Wing. But, such violence had been displayed in a wide variety of very different circumstances; its mere employment did not in any way constitute a common behavioural or social link between the men. Their reactions to prison were as diverse as their criminal backgrounds, and could only be understood by reference to the distinctive meanings of their pre-prison lives rather than extrapolated from generalizations about their dominant concerns with such undifferentiated matters as theft or violence.

We are interested firstly in this chapter in personal styles of adaptation to prison life. There are only a couple of accounts we can turn to for help in this matter. One of these is Maurice Farber's attempt to correlate particular criminal types with certain characteristics they displayed within prison.[3] It is simplest to set this out as a diagram.

CRIMINAL CHARACTERISTICS	CHARACTERISTICS AS A PRISONER			
	Trouble-someness. (1 = most trouble-some)	Suffering (1 = most suffering)	Level of Prison job (1 = best job)	Possibilities of Escape
Youthful Aggressive Lacks crystallized criminal ideology . . . no high skill . . . but daring.	1	2	5	High
Professional. Skilled Makes a living from crime. Cooperates with a group.	5	1	2	High
Habitual. Frequent involvement but lacks skill and group identity. Ideology disorganized	2	4	3	High
Neurotic. No external incentives. Crime may be symbolic.	3	5	1	Low
Situational. Little premeditation. Crime committed under pressure of extraordinary events. Respectful of authority.	4	3	4	Low

The numbers in columns 1, 2 and 3 indicate the rank order of the ratings, so that in column 1, for example, we find that the 'youthful aggressive' type was rated *most troublesome* inside prison. Farber does not give figures for column 4 so two degrees of possibility of escape are given instead.

3. Maurice Farber in Kurt Lewin (ed.), *Studies in Authority and Frustration*, op. cit.

Farber's study is conceptually appealing in that it does not divide criminals according to type of crime but according to motivational and career characteristics. There is no reference for example to violence or theft as defining characteristics of the criminal types. There are also some interesting insights contained in the correlational analysis. Situational and neurotic types for example do not try to escape; neurotic types do not suffer as much as others and it is they who tend to acquire good prison jobs. The youthful aggressive criminal on the other hand is very troublesome to the authorities, has a poor job and a high escape score.

A more recent attempt at dealing with criminal career and prison adaptation appears in John Irwin's book *The Felon*.[4] Irwin concentrates more upon the styles of prison adaptation than upon the pre-prison characteristics of those who adopt particular styles, but he does explicitly make the association between the two elements. He distinguishes three styles – doing time, jailing and gleaning. The first two of these relate back to the 'thief subculture' and the 'convict subculture' which we discussed before. Doing time is an adaptation favoured by those who 'still keep their commitment to the outside life and see prison as a suspension of that life'. It involves avoiding trouble, forming few friendships and getting out as soon as possible. Jailing involves cutting oneself off from the outside world and attempting to construct a life in prison. Finally, gleaning is an adaptation made by those who try to effect changes in their lives and identities in prison so that their future life will be different. It involves bettering or improving oneself through study or training. It is fairly evident that it will be professional thieves who favour doing time. They have a strong involvement in outside life, a circle of friends, and an occupational career pattern in which prison represents an unfortunate setback. On the other hand those who favour the jailing adaptation are men who lack such subcultural links outside. These are chiefly the group Irwin calls

4. John Irwin, *The Felon*, (Englewood Cliffs, N.J., Prentice Hall, 1970).

'state-raised' youths, those who have graduated to prison from a variety of penal institutions and whose crimes have lacked any consistent pattern or group support. Prison is a world they know and one in which they can make out and acquire status. Those who resort to gleaning suggests Irwin, will be principally drawn from the hustlers and the dope fiends.

Both Farber and Irwin make some meaningful links between outside criminal characteristics and inside adaptations. Farber suggests, for example, that the youthful aggressive type is a person who has typically taken on authority in a frontal rather than a covert manner and that this obviously relates to his preference for escape tactics once he is imprisoned. Irwin shows that the thief does time because he is part of a viable social world in which he can regularly obtain status and rewards. Involving himself with prison life therefore becomes unnecessary for his self identity. Given the diversity of the men in E-Wing, what type of links can we make between criminal careers and prison adaptations?

It is always tedious for the reader to have to plough through reservations – so perhaps we can just quickly say that our typology is based upon small numbers (five less than the forty who formed Farber's sample); it is impressionistic in that it is based on biographies and court reports rather than upon systematic interviewing; the categories are not mutually exclusive, they do not encompass all the men we know, and we do not suggest in any way that the styles of adaptation are permanent or even exclusively restricted to the types of men who at present favour them. Indeed, it is critical to our argument that over time certain adaptations will be favoured in that they represent the only workable ways of dealing with the accumulating problems of life inside.

Five Ways of Taking on Authority

Our first problem is the characterization of the men's differing criminal careers. We tried to use Farber's and Irwin's classifications and considered other typologies of criminals available in the literature. But none of these differentiated adequately between the men we knew. The problem was that the men in this group had all committed major – even sensational crimes – but crimes of a very different character (although many of them involved some form of violence). We eventually realized that the sensational nature of the crimes committed could be our starting place. These men were special in that they had hardly 'drifted' into the crime for which they were imprisoned. In most cases it would have been difficult for them to say that they did not know what they were doing when they committed the offence, for the offence was typically a very flagrant breach of social rules. In some way or another these men had taken on authority in a very serious way for at least a short period of their lives. This then led us to differentiate them by *the nature of their relationships with authority*. When they had engaged in rule breaking, to what extent was this in the face of authority, or to what extent behind authority's back?

In the first group we place those who have been involved in direct confrontation. These were the men whose criminal careers involved dramatic armed robberies, sudden and daring bank raids and hold-ups. These men carried weapons and had used them. They worked with other men but they did not have a regular group of companions. Inside prison, they were the ones most likely to engage in escape attempts or to take a leader's role in riots or demonstrations. (Our Eccleston sample referred to them as 'cowboys'.) Authority was to be directly challenged through the combined power of the prisoners. Their style of prison adaptation was obviously a carry-over from their outside authority relations. Their way of fighting back involved *confronting* although the chances of their making any impact upon authority were considerably less inside than outside. They actively resisted 'adjustment'. Piri Thomas expresses this viewpoint vividly.

I'm not gonna get institutionalized. I don't want to lose my hatred of this damn place. Once you lose your hatred, then the can's got you. You can do all the time in the world and it doesn't bug you. You can go outside and you make it; you return to prison and you make it there too. No sweat, no pain. No. Outside is real; inside is a lie. Outside is the kind of life and inside is another. And you make them the same if you lose your hate of prison.[5]

In contrast to these men were those whose relationship with authority in their criminal careers had been more *symbiotic*. Their actions had a semi-legal status; they engaged in business frauds and in protection rackets. They would claim that their frauds and protection were virtually legitimate take-overs or insurance deals. The law was not confronted but evaded. Authority was circumvented. These men had often been involved in court cases and had many times been acquitted. Evidence was hard to find against them because of the size of the network in which they operated and because their style of dealing with authority opened the way for corruption of the police. They worked for long periods with the same people, they had a stable area (or manor) in which to practise and members of the family were frequently involved in branches of their enterprise.

Within prison this group maintained close links with outside. The maintenance of relationships with family and friends was a dominant concern and therefore these men were particularly distressed by the tightening up of the visiting regulations. Their favoured style of prison adaptation was that which we described in the last chapter as campaigning. Their long association with the law meant that they had some confidence in finding ways round it. They wrote to civil servants and to M.P.s and used their wives and friends in attempts to rally support and sympathy for their cause. Sometimes wives and others went to extreme lengths in order to bring problems being experienced by the prisoners to the attention of the authorities. Despite the seriousness of the campaigns there was some occasional joking at the expense of those faceless bureaucrats

5. Piri Thomas, *Down These Mean Streets*, (New York, Alfred Knopf, 1967).

who had been forced out of their offices in order to cope in a face-to-face way with groups of vocal and well-informed callers who had refused to be fobbed off by the desk clerk.

The security wing also contained a group of men who could best be described simply as thieves. Their relationship with authority was that of 'cat and mouse', or, perhaps 'cops and robbers'. This is not to say that such men deliberately allowed themselves to be caught. They are not playing the type of game of 'cops and robbers' which Eric Berne has described and in which the player does not get his pay-off unless he is caught.[6] Nevertheless these men are happy to have the nature of their exploits known as long as they are able to keep in the background. They are pleased to pose problems for the police but this does not mean that they also carry a secret death wish. They enjoyed the game but were intent upon winning. The best words to describe their relationships with authority are *trumping* and *outflanking*. Both sides recognize that there is a contest of wits involved and that he who wins will do so by playing the cleverest card or by making the boldest move.

These were men who led relatively respectable lives outside, running shops in the suburbs, maintaining good relationships with their neighbours, but who occasionally got together with a group of specialists to carry out a major job. These were the traditional professional career thieves. They had a respect for the law which was quite different to that held by those who had confronted authority or attempted to buy it off. Their adaptation to prison tended to be fairly passive. Their problem in E-Wing was that they could hardly take the typical 'thief's' subcultural solution and do time for they faced sentences of such a length that renewal of their career upon leaving prison seemed an unlikely prospect. They had few affinities with other more confrontationalist criminals and were therefore pushed into a rather unhappy conformity to prison routines.

6. Eric Berne, *Games People Play*, (Penguin, 1970).

They allowed themselves to be interested – if not absorbed – by the daily routine; they kept to the rules and even risked incurring the annoyance of their fellow prisoners by so doing. They believed of course that they could resist the worst consequences of full retreatism but they were caught in the dilemma of needing an adaptation in order to reduce the fears engendered by the environment, but at the same time finding that the only adaptation which appealed to them was one which at times compounded such fears.

A fourth group of prisoners had avoided all confrontation with authority in their criminal lives. This was principally made up of the relatively isolated individuals who had persistently committed acts of sexual deviance in private or domestic contexts. The highly individual and private nature of their lives and acts makes it difficult to characterize their relationship with authority. External authority was probably less important than inner. These were men who felt themselves to have experienced inner compulsions, who had wrestled with their conscience, who in many instances evidenced guilt about their actions. They did not take on authority, or seek to circumvent or outwit it, they sinned against it, and even in cases where guilt was absent the sense of sin – 'the piquancy of evil' – was an element to take account of in any description of their behaviour. The term *private sinner* may therefore be the most appropriate for these men. At the very most, they had enjoyed the companionship of only one other person. Within the prison these men maintained their individualism. They engaged in such solitary occupations as hobbies involving collecting (botanical slides, film books, plants) or in reading. Their acts of aggression were likely to be solitary rather than collective, directed at one other person (more probably a fellow inmate than a staff member) rather than at authority in general. Hunger strikes which occurred in this group were undertaken by individuals over specific personal issues, rather than collectively by a group acting out of mutual self-interest. Contact with outside was negligible.

A final group of *situational* criminals (Farber's term) remains.

These men had suddenly found themselves caught up in an intolerable situation and committed a crime in order to extricate themselves from it. They had no career into which the crimes fitted and it was not therefore surprising to find that their styles of adaptation in prison showed no common pattern. But this, of course, did not mean that they did not have a style of adaptation.

Ideologies

This type of analysis of careers and adaptations at least allows us to get away from an insulated approach to prison culture which does not recognize the influence of biographies and contemporary opportunities. But a mere listing of these types of behaviour is still inadequate unless we also allow the importance of some underlying ideology. When we comment upon a particular individual's behaviour in everyday life we ascribe an ideology to him which serves as a causal string upon which to thread a variety of apparently related actions. We observe his predilection for wild nights out, for overt immorality, and meaningfully relate this to any periodic bouts of guilt by reference to his Roman Catholicism. This is not to say that his various acts are determined by his ideology, but rather that they can be understood by reference to it. More importantly, we can use an ideology to explain inconsistencies in an individual's behaviour. The authoritarianism that we observe in one who declares himself to be vitally concerned with the democratic rights of the poor and the suffering may be understood by describing his ideological affinities with Stalinism. The peculiar blend of nationalism and socialist idealism we observe in another may be united under the ideological umbrella of Zionism.

The diversity of the ideologies which men refer to can be lost sight of by sticking to such concepts as inmate culture and criminal culture in order to explain differences in adaptation to prison. Although Irwin was concerned with just such matters he could hardly miss the significance of a relatively new and highly self-conscious ideological support when he interviewed some of his prison subjects. As one black told him:

> All these years, man, I been stealing and coming to this joint. I never stopped to think why I was doing it. I thought that all I wanted was money and stuff. You know, man, now I can see why I thought the way I did. I been getting fucked up all my life and never realized it. The white man has been telling me that I should want his stuff. But he didn't give me no way to get it. Now I ain't going for his shit anymore. I'm a Black man. I'm going to get out of here and see what I can do for my people. I'm going to do what I have to do to get those white mother-fuckers off my people's back.[7]

In this example we can clearly see the way in which theft and prison are suddenly given a new meaning by the adoption of a particular ideology, but this is not all. This ideology when it is present in an extreme situation such as prison can be called upon for *help*. We may even decide that the validity of an ideology rests upon its ability to help us through extreme situations. It is quite common to hear atheists being warned that their ideology will not be as useful to them in the 'hour of need', unlike Christianity or some other religious ethic. Admiral Byrd catches this point perfectly when he describes his long, isolated days in the arctic as an occasion for determining the 'pay levels' of particular philosophies. His own physical abilities are important for endurance, but he knows that he must also draw continually upon his inner philosophical stock.

> Where there is no growth or change outside, men are driven deeper and deeper inside themselves for materials of replenishment. And on these hidden levels of self replenishment, which might be called the pay levels of philosophy, would depend the ability of any group of men to outlast such an ordeal and not come to hate each other.[8]

We recognize that monks, hermits and ascetics need not necessarily have 'guts' but they should know how to draw on

7. Irwin, *The Felon*, p. 63.
8. Richard Byrd, *Alone*, (London, Putnam, 1938), p. 151.

their own resources and be inward looking people from the beginning. Such props are not so much internal ones derived from the personality, but more the exterior strengths of a particular ideological loyalty. We don't know much about the personal qualities which helped Jackson, the British ambassador held in captivity by the Tupamaros; we do know that he was sustained by some feeling of patriotism, a conviction that the British Government would never let him down. Similarly Anthony Grey, the Reuter correspondent, kept in Peking for a number of years, recorded that he was kept going by the knowledge that the Foreign Office was doing everything possible to obtain his release. Both Jackson and Grey could resist the attacks on themselves through their patriotism and belief in the British way of life: in other words by reference to a sustaining ideology. A number of important studies on 'brain washing' in wartime and in political prisons show how significant the protective and insulative nature of personal ideologies and convictions are. We take it for granted that religion helps people sustain long fasts, and extreme physical deprivation. Thus Robin Knox-Johnston, the round-the-world boatsman, observed that 'throughout the voyage I never really felt I was completely alone, and I think a man would have to be inhumanly confident and self-reliant if he were to make this sort of voyage without belief in God'.[9]

Similarly political detainees, exiles in labour camps, and even polar explorers may be maintained by their commitment to particular ideals. But do such commitments always help and are some of more help than others? To answer such questions it is not enough to know about the self selective mechanisms which send strong people into jungles, convinced people into monasteries. We must know what happens when a range of very different people get forced into the same situation.

One series of studies that contains groups large enough for comparisons to be made is the work on concentration camps.

9. Robin Knox-Johnston, *A World of My Own*, (London, Cassell, 1969), p. 173.

Bettelheim, for example, has analysed inmate reactions in terms of two rather straight-forward categories, socio-economic class and political education.[9] He found that the politically educated prisoners found support for their self-esteem in the fact that the Gestapo had singled them out as important enough to take revenge upon. Their imprisonment demonstrated how dangerous they had been and this helped them in withstanding at least the initial psychological shock. Bettelheim also talks about how some political prisoners could endure the camp because the punishment alleviated the guilt they had felt about failing to prevent the Nazi rise to power.

The non-political middle-class prisoners on the other hand had no such prop: they were unable to cope with the shock; 'they found themselves utterly unable to comprehend what happened to them ... they had no consistent philosophy that would protect their integrity as human beings'. They had always obeyed the law, now the law was apparently being turned against them: it must all be a mistake, they could not be treated 'like ordinary criminals'. Eventually they realized the actual situation and they were the prisoners, according to Bettelheim, who disintegrated the quickest. Suicides were practically confined to this group and later their behaviour was the most anti-social and shiftless.

The upper-class prisoners were again somewhat different. They segregated themselves from others, seemed unable to accept what was happening but (unlike the middle-class and like the kidnapped ambassador) seemed convinced that they would be released within the shortest time because of their importance. 'In order to endure life in the camp they developed such a feeling of superiority that nothing could touch them.' Bettelheim summarizes his general point in this way:

It seems that most prisoners tried to protect themselves against the initial shock by mustering forces helpful in supporting their

10. Bruno Bettelheim, 'Individual and Mass Behaviour in Extreme Situations', *Journal of Abnormal and Social Psychology*, XXXVIII (1943), pp. 417–52.

badly shaken self-esteem. Those groups which found in their past life some basis for the erection of such a buttress to their endangered egos seemed to succeed.

Bettelheim is here referring to initial shock and we have already noted that the stripping and initiation rites which mark the entrance to a total institution are not reacted to with equal stress. It is not difficult to predict that someone with a long history of periods in a children's home, approved school, Borstal, and army camp will find the shock of institutional life less acute than the naïve newcomer. What we cannot predict with any certainty are the eventual long-term patterns of adaptation. Some ideologies, for example, the religious ones, might indeed sustain someone beyond the initial shock stage for an almost indefinite period. In other cases the ideological buttresses might simply crumble leaving the individual even more vulnerable to disintegration because his previous source of superiority over others has failed him. There are not enough accounts of periods longer than a few years to know whether this happens. More often we find something like the reverse: the ideology is discovered – through prolonged self-examination, reading, conversion by another believer – some time after the person has been struggling. Well-documented examples include Eldridge Cleaver's conversion to the Black Muslim creed in Folsom Prison, Genet's transformation (into actor, martyr, and saint – in Sartre's various characterizations) after years in French prison and (more ambiguously, because of the unknowns about his initial motivation) Lawrence of Arabia's various 'conversions' in the desert. We cannot predict directions. We can only say that sustaining ideologies are crucial to survival in extreme situations.

To show the potency of certain ideologies or philosophies as aids to survival – whether brought into the prison or acquired during a sentence – let us give four examples from different types of American prisoners over the last decade.

The first is the type of commitment found in groups such as

the 'freedom riders' imprisoned for their civil rights activities in the south at the beginning of the sixties. One such activist describes how a group of freedom riders imprisoned in an isolated maximum security unit in a southern prison, drew on their political and religious commitment to develop what he calls 'ecstatic solidarity'.[11] The group brought into the unit a high sense of morale, an outrage at the 'mistaken identity' involved in being treated as dangerous felons, and the knowledge that 'we were in fact carrying out our political objectives by simply filling the jails'. They could thus counteract the damaging definitions they faced and minimize those pains of interaction we described in Chapter Three. Their main method of inducing ecstatic solidarity was through collective singing of hymns, folk and civil rights songs. Martinson describes the cumulative effect: 'At last we were together, in one body, communicants in common activity, bound together by ties which did not bind and were not painful. We were completely together and completely adjusted to the rules of maximum security.'

An allied, but perhaps more intellectually calculated and active type of sustaining ideology, can be found in the writings of a later group of American political prisoners: conscientious objectors, and those imprisoned for draft resistance and opposition to the American involvement in Vietnam. Two such war resisters, Howard Levy and David Miller, have written a training manual for this type of prisoner, telling him what to expect inside, how to comprehend the system and how to continue the fight while incarcerated. They assume that if such 'moral witnesses' are to survive and even make good use of this time, they must appreciate all aspects of the prison: religion, visits, friendships, psychiatry, homosexuality, work, censorship, how to treat the guards. They state explicitly: 'Political education and prison resistance form the cornerstone of an

11. Robert Martinson, 'Prison Notes of a Freedom Rider', *The Nation*, 194 (1962) and *Social Interaction Under Close Confinement*, (Institute for Social Sciences, University of California, Berkeley, 1966).

effective and sanity-preserving approach to imprisonment.'[12]
They distinguish such resistance – as we did – from the routine
ways of coping by immersing oneself in the underlife of the
prison. They concede that even if the political sucess of such
resistance (for example, in undermining the morale of the armed
forces) was not clear . . . 'it is certain that our spirit of struggle
was of inestimable value in maintaining our own morale at a
high level'.[13]

A third and altogether different approach to prison life can
be found in the sustaining ideologies evolved by those in a
hippie, mystical or drug-related orbit who find themselves in
prison. One guru of this movement, Timothy Leary, provides
an articulate statement in his *Jail Notes*.[14] A clue to his survival
can be found in Allen Ginsberg's perface describing how Leary
had made 'an exquisite religious covenant in jail'. The jail
notes are full of references to such sources of sustenance as the
Upanishads – which, Leary tells a cell mate, 'hath many a soul
freed incarceration'[15] – and the ways in which the prison experience could be seen in a more positive light, even as a
'revelatory event':

Prison cell perfect experimental psychology laboratory. Locked
in single cell, with me own mind, me own body. Soulitary confinement.

Stimulus deprivation. Outside, we ricochet each day through
billion-faceted traffic-jam of choice points. Inside single cell
choice restricted. What do with body? What do with mind?
Hermetic purity. Monastic vacuum void external pressure.

Crazed minotaur chained in centre of complex maze. Letters
restricted. Visits restricted. No phone calls. Foreign relations so

12. Howard Levy and David Miller, *Going to Jail: The Political
Prisoner*, (New York, Grove Press, 1971, p. 87).
13. ibid., p. 170.
14. Timothy Leary, *Jail Notes*, (New York, Douglas Books, 1970).
15. The cell mate's response to this advice is not recorded, although
by all accounts, Leary was very popular in prison and even made some
converts.

rare so slow observe effects microscopic clear. In-communication.[16]

The final, sustaining ideology – one which we have often referred to – is at the opposite pole of Leary's mystical trip: the radical, primarily black, political ideology. This is too complex to characterize in a few words, but at least these elements can be identified: the prison is a microcosm of wider society, a concentrated form of the repressive power of the state; the prisoners are (in various versions) slaves, victims of racism, rejects of capitalism or even the objects of a socially planned genocide policy. Leaving aside all questions about its political potential and the real help it provides for collective problems (civil rights, legal protection), the movement clearly offers a powerful and all encompassing sustaining ideology for the individual. A frequently quoted interchange with a black prisoner negotiating in a New York prison mutiny in 1970 went like this:

Q. What is your name.
A. I am a revolutionary.
Q. What are you charged with.
A. I was born black.
Q. How long have you been in.
A. I've had troubles since the day I was born.

The definitive and most eloquent statement of this ideology is provided by the person who died defending it, George Jackson. His prison letters have become the bible of the movement, and we select from them two typical statements: 'Very few men imprisoned for economic crimes or even crimes of passion against the oppressor feel that they are really guilty', and further:

There are still some blacks here who consider themselves criminal but not many. Believe me, my friend, with the time these brothers have to read, study, and think, you will find no class or category more aware, more embittered, desperate or

16. Leary, *Jail Notes*, pp. 44–5.

dedicated to the ultimate remedy – revolution. The most dedicated, the best of our kind – you find them in the Folsoms, San
Quentins and Soledads.[17]

We can hardly ignore the potential of these and similar
ideologies – although as sociologists we have to question carefully how far they have permeated American and other prison
systems and how they are actually used on a day to day basis.
Clearly, for the E-Wing prisoners the achievement of 'ecstatic
solidarity' through hymn singing, the dedicated resistance of
moral witnesses, a place in Leary's mind experiments or in
George Jackson's 'implacable army of liberation' are not the
immediately available alternatives. We must now therefore
relate the notion of sustaining ideologies more specifically to
the group of men we knew in Durham. This means asking
the following questions:

1. What ideologies are known or available to the men in E-
Wing?

2. How does such availability vary according to the personal
biography of each prisoner?

3. Which ideology is likely to be chosen or found most useful
in terms of survival?

Our argument so far has been that we cannot explain adaptation to long-term imprisonment by simply referring to an
inmate subculture, we also need reference to the personal and
externally manifested behavioural characteristics of the men
who make up the security wing's population. They have contrasting relationships to authority outside the prison and these
are related to adaptive styles inside. In addition, we found a
need to know about the ideologies which informed such styles,
the belief systems which gave meaning to the life inside and
outside prison.

Consider firstly the man whose relationship with external
authority has involved direct confrontation. His philosophy of

17. George Jackson, *Soledad Brother*, (Penguin, 1971, pp. 30 and
31).

life is referred to in his general statements about life and the world. The world is out there and consists of people who 'had it coming to them'. Success in life involves going out and getting your share; it necessitates dare-devil techniques – the bank raid, the armed robbery – and it means working against the odds much of the time but in this challenge one confirms oneself. Life has to be lived dramatically or not at all and crime provided the opportunity for taking dramatic chances. It was like the racetrack to a racing driver, a dangerous life which could not be made safer without losing its possibilities for confirmation of self. To men of this orientation prison was another challenge. The escape was now the behaviour which ran against the odds and was therefore eagerly attempted.

These elements are tied together by their common links with the ideology of romantic anarchism.

The behaviour of such criminals contains the distinctive blend of recklessness, anti-authoritarianism and egoism which has characterized many of the political bandits celebrated in films and novels. Victor Serge writing of the anarchist Bonnot Gang in Paris in the 1900s which was eventually wiped out by executions and police bullets after a succession of daring bank robberies and murders, compares the gang and its followers to an earlier anarchist phase in France.[18]

The same psychological features and the same social factors were present in both phases; the same exacting idealism in the breasts of uncomplicated men whose energy could find no outlet in achieving a higher dignity or sensibility, because any such outlet was physically denied to them. Conscious of their frustration, they battled like madmen and were beaten down.

Serge describes the brief lives of those 'outlaw-anarchists'. They 'shot at the police and blew out their own brains. Others, overpowered before they could fire the last bullet into their own heads, went off sneering to the guillotine'. 'One against all.' 'Nothing means anything to me.'

The brief almost hysterical sense of power and freedom

18. Victor Serge, *Memoirs of a Revolutionary*.

which such sentiments can bring when they inform a series of illegal acts was well caught in the violence and laughter of the American film 'Bonnie and Clyde'.[19]

The massive popularity of this film and of goods and records associated with it was undoubtedly related to the general appeal of the romantic anarchism of its heroes, their absurd bravery in the face of hopeless odds. Even the particularly violent ending which was much criticized by film critics, fitted the ideology of this particular life style. Bonnot, the French anarchist, was besieged for a day before being shot to bits by police bullets as he lay between two mattresses. After his death popular songs and stories referred romantically to the 'bandit tragique'.

None of this means that the confrontationist criminal is really a political rebel. We are not claiming that the men we have met are like Bonnot, but only that their ideas of life can be successfully tied together with reference to an ideology which also informs the behaviour of many political rebels. Their own belief systems do occasionally come into direct alignment with the ideas behind romantic anarchism, but often they contain other elements drawn from such contrasting ideologies as utilitarianism and asceticism. Basic to the criminal type we have described and to the romantic anarchist is the the idea that life cannot be lived fully within present society, and that one can only make out by taking on orthodox society in a direct manner. The following passage, taken from Chris's letter from which we have already quoted in a different context has these elements as recurrent themes:

The lynchpin of this ideology [the criminal's] is an ethos based on courage and the commitment to it by risk taking in the quest for prestige and self-esteem ranging from epitomizing gladiator virtues to challenging authority. Individuals that combine this ethos with a lack of identification in the mores and values of

19. For an account of the real Bonnie and Clyde and other 'cowboys without horses', see Lew Louderback *Pretty Boy, Baby Face – I Love You,* (New York, Fawcett Publications, 1968).

society have the option of investing or exploiting the resulting primitive ideology in property crime or gansterism. The code of conduct regulating intra-criminality is based on analogues of courage-loyalty, staunchness-bravery; however successfully the criminal enshrines them is irrelevant, these virtues constitute the basis of his code.

The writer, as we shall see when we compare his account with that given by other criminals, is in fact describing the ideology of only one group of criminals rather than all criminals, although he evidently considers that it is the latter task which engages him. The specificity of his ideology is epitomized in the following extract from the same letter.

Once one can accept risk-taking and involve one's self-esteem in measuring up to it then its dangers are like the possibility of getting gored to the bullfighter or crashing to the racing-driver . . . Imprisonment is part of the game.

In much the same way, one might add, as the guillotine or the police bullet was 'part of the game' to the French anarchists.

The confrontationist criminal considers himself an outsider. Serge captures the self-defeating nature of this 'revolutionary stance' when he sadly observes of the French anarchists: 'they did not stop to think that society has no fringe, that no one is ever outside it, even in the depths of the dungeons, and that their "conscious egoism" . . . linked up with the most brutal bourgeois individualism'.

Those who adopt elements of romantic anarchism as an ideology nevertheless set themselves off from society as a self-conscious policy, and in this they differ from the symbiotic criminals who subscribe to an ideology which involves the subversion rather than the overthrow of society, the bending and fixing and rigging of rules rather than the flouting of them. They do not battle against the odds but rather make certain that they control the outcomes in such a way as to maximize their winnings. Their lives are not dramatically conceived; when they are caught they philosophically observe that it could easily have been otherwise, that they were unlucky, that the 'police had to get them for something'. They are anxious to stress their behavioural similarities to others rather than their differences – for after all as they frequently claim with reference to their deviance – 'everybody does it'. This group subscribes to an ideology which can be called without too much irony *innovative capitalism*. There are many accounts of the behaviour which can be subsumed under this heading, but few of the ideology. Edward Alsworth Ross however does justice to the belief system of this criminal in his characterization of what he calls the 'criminaloid'.[20] Criminaloids, he writes, are not 'degenerates tormented by monstrous cravings. They want nothing more than we all want – money, power, consideration – in a word, success; but they are in a hurry and they are not particular as to the means'. This type does not confront but rather relies upon others. 'Conscious of the antipodal difference between doing wrong and getting it done, he places out his 'dirty work'. Neither is the criminaloid anti-social.

Within his home town, his ward, his circle, he is perhaps a good man judged by the simple old-time texts. Very likely he keeps his marriage vows, pays his debts, 'mixes' well, stands by his friends and has a contracted kind of public spirit. He is ready enough to rescue imperilled babies, protect maidens or help poor widows. He is unevenly moral: Oak in the family and clan virtues, but basswood in commercial and civic ethics.

The symbiotic criminal may even regard himself as the conservative protector of the local community against the in-roads of the state. Again in Ross's words he 'plays the support of his local or special group against the larger society . . . He is the champion of the tribal order as opposed to the civil order'. The law which stands outside his local community is not an object of intrinsic oppression; it is 'a club to rescue your friends from and to smite your enemies with, but it has no claim of its own'. The symbiotic criminal regards it as malleable. He

20. Edward Alsworth Ross, 'The Criminaloid', in Gilbert Geis (ed.) *White Collar Criminal*, (New York, Atherton Press, 1968).

cannot see why everything may not be 'arranged', 'settled out of court'.

It is a compound of these elements of local morality, and community support which make up the capitalistic self-righteousness of the symbiotic criminal. 'In the dusk and the silence [of public opinion] the magic of clan opinion converts his misdeeds into something rich and strange.' His capitalistic ideology can even become publicly admired, his legal derelictions come to be seen as public services. He can declare himself to be a more fundamental and thoroughgoing businessman than others. 'He invokes a psuedo-Darwinism to sanction the revival of outlawed and bygone tactics of struggle . . . To win the game with the aid of a sleeveful of aces proves one's fitness to survive.'

The persistence of this ideology within the prison is to be seen in the way in which such symbiotic deviants continually argue and debate with the Home Office and its officials through their own letters and the personal intervention of their relations. The idea that there is a way in which matters can be sorted out or arranged dies hard.

The confrontationist and symbiotic offenders have fairly well defined relationships to the world of law and authority. But the man who concentrates upon trumping or outflanking has not. He raids the world of property and those who control it in much the same way as the international oil company's executive (stylized in the T.V. *Troubleshooters* of Mogul) descends on new countries to scheme for their mineral wealth. He is at home or aspires to be at home in the world of the international set; when on the run he gravitates to the south of France rather than south London and if his occupation were legal he would be the perfect target for the Rothman's 'International' advertisements. His 'front' will be antique dealer rather than scrap merchant. His origins are much the same as those of the other types we have described, but in Robert Merton's terms he is a 'cosmopolitan' rather than a 'local'. He shares with the confrontationist a taste for drama and excitement, but the action does not need the edge of desperation which the confrontationist gives it. His orientation to leisure values is hedonistic, but he is a cool rather than a tough hedonist.

He is essentially professional in that his jobs are planned with considerable ingenuity and executive skill. But the Raffles 'gentleman criminal' air he sometimes cultivates, his distaste for the heavy stuff and his eventual aspiration to retire on the proceeds of the 'one really big one', make him somewhat of an outsider to the criminal subculture and its prison variant. When he finds himself trapped in prison he is only half prepared for it, and his despair and depression is often deep. His previous encounters with authority have been transitory and he has often been smart enough to win. Now – like a Mogul man held hostage on a deserted island – most previous forms of adaptation are unsuitable. More than the other E-Wing prisoners he puts some faith in the authorities such as the Parole Board, and otherwise looks for sustaining ideologies in the literature of the self-imposed romantic exile – Fitzgerald in the Paris of the Jazz Age, early American bohemians, or testimonies about those who are never at home, who manifest unease: from Hesse's *Steppenwolf* to 'Marlowe treading softly down some mean street of L.A.'

It is only possible to describe the ideology of our next group, the private sinners, by sticking at a low level of abstraction. We must be careful not to speak too generally about a very heterogeneous group. Unlike the others we have described in this section, sexual deviants have no community of fellow deviants in which they operate and in which they can establish a consensual view of society or of social control. It would be absurd to apply words like capitalist or anarchist or utilitarian to their belief systems, for their particular type of deviance is not capable of description by reference to such particular worldly ideologies or to compounds of them. In fact the world out there is of relatively little significance. These men tend to live within their own heads; their own thoughts preoccupy them. They do not want to take on the world in any way, they have no apparent desire for power or wealth, their obsessions are not widely held goals but private fantasies. In Farber's words 'These men did not commit crime because they could not make an economic adjustment to society; they committed them in spite of this ability.' Their eventual deviance results from a reliance upon their inner compulsion, upon a belief that they have no other course but to follow their inner promptings. This inner reliance has most affinity with certain religious attitudes, with certain forms of mysticism, in that the individual comes to be dominated by concerns about himself and his own desires. The necessity of coming to terms with his own beliefs and desires becomes more important than the problem of relationship with the external world. He is involved, in Weber's terms, in a 'flight from the world'. This is not to say that the sexual deviant does not make plans or act rationally in the pursuit of goals – there is good evidence that many of the most apparently impulsive acts involve both these elements – but rather to emphasize the relatively high degree of self-immersion which is forced upon this type of person by virtue of the private and highly personal nature of his relationship with others in the world. To draw upon Weber's description of the mystic in an unusual context we may say that the sexual deviant is 'in' the world and 'externally accommodates to its orders' but this very act of accommodating to the world is regarded as the resistance to temptation: the world provides a series of situations in which fantasies can be internally preserved or behaviourally enacted with tragic consequences. Giving in to a temptation is not justified by reference to the nature of the external world but rather by reference to the extreme nature of the inner compulsion.

Within prison we observe an intensification of the inner-worldliness of this group of deviants. The favoured pursuits are those in which success is entirely a matter for personal assessment and reinforcement. Whereas amongst other groups there may be some indulgence in competitive hobbies like weight-lifting or toy-making, amongst this group we observed a preference for collecting. Martin collected botanical slides and Peter collected magazines dealing with the history of the film. Of course this stress upon self-maintenance was not a simple product of continued adherence to an external belief system in which self-consciousness played a significant part. Inner-worldliness and social isolation were forced upon these men by the type of social considerations that we have outlined earlier. Nevertheless our discussions with them did suggest that they enjoyed an ability to live within their own world; they did not, even after a considerable period of physical proximity, appear to constitute any sort of open community in which different world-views could be paraded or discussed.

Which Ideologies Work?

Up to this point our account of ideologies has been rather simple-minded. We have said that particular ideologies may be said to inform distinctive criminal life styles and that such ideologies also influence adaptation to long-term imprisonment. But this is only half the story. For of course we must also consider the extent to which particular ideologies *work* within prison. One may need the ideological strut of romantic anarchism to carry out daring bank raids, the neo-Darwinian belief in innovative capitalism in order to sustain one's semi-legal involvement in protection rackets; one may need a feeling of cool hedonism to inform the planning of a jewel theft and a sense of inner compulsion to justify the sexual crime, but how do such philosophies make out in the prison, how well do they sustain one during years inside?

The anti-authoritarianism of the confrontationist criminal is not an ideology which enjoys any long-term success. Maurice Farber describes the gradual attenuation of this philosophy:

An aggressive young criminal is convicted of some crime of violence and given a long sentence. The situation appears hopeless to him; he has little to lose. Nor does he have much respect for the authorities. He attempts escape ... usually the escape attempt fails. For a few years he is badly behaved, rebelling against the authority of the prison and often continuing to plot escape. There may be something of a tapering off in his bad behaviour as it becomes obvious through bitter experience that it can get him no place.

The individual whose relationship with authority is less confrontationist may enjoy more ideological reinforcement. There is always a slight chance that some aspect of the prison system can be subverted, some way in which rules can be bent. Every opportunity has to be exploited and even in the most overtly authoritarian situation, the possibility of a loophole exists as the following extracts from an autobiographical essay suggest. The object of the author's devious attentions in this passage is not the Home Office but the British Army.

I eventually arrived at the last doctor, who asked me if I had ever suffered from various diseases, or been in hospital. I thought 'this is my chance' if I fail my medical. I said 'Yes. I was in a bad motor accident – in hospital for a week and have suffered from bad headaches and dizzy spells ever since.' I was told to wait outside until my name was called. After some time my name was called and I was given a card which said I passed A.1.

On his first day in the Army Jock tried another tactic when he refused to sign the Official Secrets Act.

Would you give information away to the Russians? [demands the commanding officer] I said 'fucking right I would if given half the chance'. By this time there was quite a crowd. I thought maybe I could get out of the army like this. He said, 'Don't be silly – you don't mean that.' I said, 'Of course I do – why should I fight for this capitalist country?'

After this particular tactic has failed, Jock resorted to feigning illness:

I was looking for a way out [he was on his way to the guard-house] when the sergeant in charge said 'Don't you feel well?' With this as my cue, I fainted. I was given water, sat in a chair, someone sent for tea for me. I told the sergeant I suffered from blackouts.

This secured his removal to hospital where he feigned madness in a further attempt to secure his release:

> After a while I quietened down and started to think of ways to show them I was mad. I had a lot of newspapers in my cell. I sat on my bed and tore them up into confetti, throwing them all over the floor; while I was doing this I saw the flap go up on the Judas hole and realized I was being observed. I decided to give them a show so I leaped off the bed and started shadow boxing.

The comic element in many of these tactics should not obscure the insistent determination to subvert the system which informs them. There is no moral or frontal challenge to authority involved – the belief is simply that there is a way around all regulations; those who beat the system are the fittest no matter what moral or physical contortions they may have to go through in the process. This ideology clearly has great staying power. Even a minor victory over a Whitehall official presumably provides some sign of the malleability of the system, some hope that it can eventually be 'bought'.

The inner-worldliness which characterizes the sexual deviants is an appealing ideology. But its dangers lie in its affinities with a vegetable-like retreatism. Mysticism is an attractive religion to those who live in a dispiriting natural environment, but the decision to take a psychic trip is bedevilled by the possibility that one's inner resources will not prove adequate for the journey – that the reflection will turn into self-pity, the contemplation into catatonia.

Perhaps the ideology which might survive least well in the security wing is the cool hedonism of the career thief. There is nothing in this belief system which helps one to face twenty years inside. Authority is not an object for attack or systematic subversion according to this philosophical position. Its legitimacy is accepted, its principles even respected. When it is flouted by criminal behaviour, then this is merely a temporary twisting of the tail, an insolent reminder of the presence of the master criminal. The game tends to break down in prison – the good life is too far away. The ideology has few elements which help one to sustain the pains of imprisonment.

We can usefully summarize the argument in this chapter schematically. Our concern has been the culture of the security wing, the peculiar mix of ideas which inform conversations and personal behaviour and influence styles of adaptation. One view of prison culture, which we can describe as the system model, assumes that the particular cultural system found in the prison arises in response to the demands of the immediate situation. It is a cultural system which is produced by the requirements of life in an institution.

The System Model

PRISON

Prison Culture arises as response to problems generated by prison life

A second model (which we may attribute to Irwin and Cressey) introduces another element – the thief culture – which is brought into the prison from outside by particular types of criminals.

The Two Culture Model

PRISON

| Criminal Career Outside. → | Inmate Culture |
| | Thief Culture |

Irwin's more complex version of this model involves taking into account the detailed career behaviour of particular criminals and then predicting from this particular styles of cultural adaptation within prison.

Nature of Pre-Prison Career

PRISON ADAPTATION

State-Raised Youth. ⟶
Hustlers and Dope Fiends. ⟶
Professional Criminals. ⟶

Jailing – Inmate Culture
Gleaning
Doing Time – Thief Culture

Finally in our tentative account we have attempted to use ideologies as a link between external and internal behaviour, characterizing the external behaviour in terms of the relationships with authority which it implies.

Characterization of Relationships with Authority Implied by Criminal Career	Typical Crime	Ideological Affinities	Adaptive Predictions
confrontational	armed robbery	romantic anarchism	rebellion and escapes
symbiotic	protection – organized crime	innovative capitalism	campaigning/ subverting
trumping/ outflanking	professional theft	cool hedonism	no style entailed ('giving in' adopted by default in some cases)
private sin	sexual deviance	inner- worldliness	mystical retreatism
situational	various	no general ideology	no style entailed

There is of course nothing fixed about this analysis and it might be only marginally relevant in prisons where any differences in previous biographies and present ideologies may be blurred by some over-riding common characteristic – such as being black.

Ideologies may be partially or totally abandoned when they fail to help adaptation, or when they became unacceptable for other reasons. New ideologies may enter the culture from outside and be taken over by inmates, although this process will be partly dependent upon the availablity of certain ideological 'props' within the prison; it would have been difficult, for example, for anyone to take up a hippie ideology a few years ago, for its adoption at that time entailed some form of drug-use. It has not been our intention in this chapter to imprison men in neat ideological boxes. The schematization we have employed does not represent the foundations of some grand predictive model, but is rather an attempt to make our argument about the complexity of E-Wing culture more apparent and to show the way in which links between pre-prison and prison life can be drawn.

CHAPTER EIGHT

Taking sides

'What good do you think you do?
Do you think that I'll be different when I'm
through?'

Johnny Cash, *Ballad of San Quentin*

We have more or less kept ourselves out of the narrative up
to this point. It should be quite obvious, though, from the
methodology we adopted and the nature of our relationships
with the men, that we have not simply played the roles of de-
tached seekers after information in this research project. Many
sociologists have now – somewhat belatedly – begun to question
the viability of such roles anyway, although they have been for
the most part notably reticent about what else they think they
are up to as they go about their research.

Whose Side Are We On?

In his rhetorically titled paper 'Whose Side Are We On?' the
American sociologist, Howard Becker, argues that it is impossible in sociological research not to be contaminated by sympathy.[1] It is not a question of whether we take sides, but whose
side we are on. As soon as we take deviant definitions seriously
and accord them some credibility, we are open to the charge of
bias – a charge, Becker notes, which doesn't arise if we simply
take over the officials' definitions. This is because of the 'hierarchy of credibility' which operates in our society, a moral
pyramid which ensures a differential distribution of the right
to be heard. Deviant groups have violated the moral order of

1. Howard S. Becker. 'Whose Side Are We On?', *Social Problems*,
14 (Winter 1967), pp. 239–47.

society and are therefore thought to have sacrificed their right to be listened to.

In fact many deviant groups are now being listened to and this moral hierarchy is being challenged by the politicization of groups such as drug takers, homosexuals, and some American prisoners. But the sort of prisoners who are in E-Wing are not among such groups: murderers, armed robbers, sexual offenders and racketeers are not exactly vocal and organized pressure groups. Nor do they have a literature and ideology which redefines their offences as political – in the way, for example, that Eldridge Cleaver was able to present his status as a rapist in ideological terms.[2] They do not write letters to the press or march in Hyde Park to defend their interests. By taking their definitions seriously – of their prison as well as their general situation – we have obviously exposed ourselves to the sort of charges which Becker describes. Certainly, as we walked into the wing each week for over three years, we found it difficult not to feel sympathy with the prisoners' situation. We were faced with a small group of individuals contained in an oppressive, highly structured environment by a monolithic force. These men are faced with the prospect of spending most of their lives in very similar circumstances. As we described in Chapter One, we found ourselves becoming friends as well as teachers of the men, and these close relationships became as important as any research commitment.

We also admitted that such involvements were by no means ambiguous. There are so many obvious areas of disjunction between our lives that it would be facile to talk about anything like full identification with the prisoners. Nor – it should be made clear – are we unaware of the dangers of sentimentality. The implications which Becker detects in the charge of bias – namely that damaging or uncomfortable findings are repressed and the deviant is released from any moral guilt which is then deflected onto society – should not be read into our commitment. One simple reason is that the men do not accept the

2. Eldridge Cleaver, *Soul on Ice*, (London, Cape, 1969).

simplistic sentimental view of themselves as victims, as more sinned against than sinning.

Our position is close to the 'appreciative' stance recommended by David Matza.[3] This involves abandoning ideas of correction, and any attempts to get rid of the deviant phenomenon, and instead favours attempts to empathize with and thus comprehend the subject of inquiry. This commitment to the phenomenon without violating its integrity has – as Matza is aware – dangers and absurdities. It means suspending some conventional standards of morality, but it also means avoiding romanticism (which is close to Becker's sentimentalism): not denying or suppressing the distasteful features of the phenomenon. Being on the men's sides was an essential part of the research endeavour. But such taking of sides does not imply anything like a blanket moral approval for what some of the men had done to get them in prison. The men themselves oscillated between wanting to convert us to certain features of their enterprise – the style and attitude, rather than the action itself – and wanting us to retain some conventional standards of morality.

Taking sides in this fashion does result in limitations. We have recorded the hostility we incurred because of the prison authorities' suspicion that we were in league with the men. This meant that we could not give any detailed description of the way in which the situation is seen by the officials. As a few writers on prisons – such as the Morrises in their study of Pentonville – have made clear, the prison officers are very much part of the prison community and we would have liked to have known how they viewed the situation. We suspect though that while in formal terms the E-Wing staff is part of the community, the unique features of E-Wing made their roles more peripheral than in an ordinary prison. Certainly the prisoners saw them as little more than irritating caretakers sent in from the outside world to administer to their daily needs and run the security and custodial arrangements. For the guards the situa-

3. David Matza, *Becoming Deviant*, (Englewood Cliffs, Prentice Hall, 1969).

tion was not extreme in the sense of imposing the same demands made on the men. They (like us) had a world outside the prison – family, colleagues, staff club, trade union – from which they could take up positions of more or less detachment towards what was happening in the wing.

For a few of the senior prison staff who were more intimately concerned with the wing this was not quite the case. Some of them became highly involved in the day-to-day life of the prisoners. This produced for at least one such official the feeling that he had more common points of discussion with the prisoners than with most of his outside acquaintances – something we have often felt ourselves. But we cannot begin to do justice to such views and we doubt whether it is possible to see both sides at the same time.

Exchanging Ideologies

David Matza, with customary eloquence, notes that:

A serious commitment to the subjective view cannot grudgingly stop with the appreciation of the subject's definition of his specific deviant predicament. It must also entail an appreciation of the ordinary subject's philosophical definition of his general predicament. Concretely, this means that the ordinary assumptions of members of society like the capacity to *transcend* circumstances, the capacity to *improvise*, the capacity to *intend* must be treated seriously and occupy a central place in the analysis of social life.[4]

Most of this book has been concerned with attempting to describe such a philosophy and we hope we have done justice to the prisoners' general as well as specifically deviant predicament. The problem with doing collaborative research such as this – and the very publication of this book – is that the philosophy has to be given back to its adherents, albeit in the partial and stylized verbal form in which we as sociologists and writers have wrapped it. What this then means is that the philosophy

4. David Matza, ibid, p. 25.

becomes one among many. It becomes open to criticism, vulnerable to attack. The sustaining fictions are seen as fictional, the self delusions become manifest.

We have not just transcribed philosophies, ideologies and views of the world: we have played some part in creating them and our commitments are such as to make us wonder whether certain ideologies can be allowed to go unchallenged when they first appear. We recognize our concern for example in trying to keep the men in a rational frame of mind, although we know full well that the rationality we seek to encourage may only be championed by us so assiduously because it more or less works for us in the outside world and fits best with our own working theories of human behaviour. So, the passive fatalistic ideology unconsciously adopted by Ivan Denisovich is one that we are conscious of opposing.[5] Here is Solzhenitsyn's description of a day in a Soviet prison camp:

Shukhov went to sleep fully content. He'd had many strokes of luck that day: they hadn't put him in the cells; they hadn't sent the team to the settlement; he got a bowl of kasha at dinner; the team-leader had fixed the rates well; he'd built a wall and enjoyed doing it; he'd smuggled that bit of hacksaw blade through; he'd earned something from Tsezar in the evening; he bought that tobacco. And he hadn't fallen ill. He'd got over it. A day without a dark cloud. Almost a happy day.

Our opposition to such an ideology is not whole-hearted. Not only have we no firm ground for being sure that this ideology will not work for at least some of the men, but we recognize that from the heterogeneity of delusional systems available to us outside the prison, we can probably select none which guarantee us much more than this limited happiness.

Despite our insecurity about the content of what we are exchanging with the prisoners, we are sure that the process of exchange is important. The transformations between levels of analysis which we described as a feature of our methodology

5. Alexander Solzhenitsyn, *One Day in the Life of Ivan Denisovich*, op. cit.

in Chapter One (from personal to literary to sociological – or the reverse) can be seen to have some therapeutic effects. It is trite enough to point out how individual predicaments and anxieties may be transformed by their association with more fully articulated ideologies. We may observe, for example, how undergraduates' personal problems are articulated by reference to Camus, Sartre or whoever else is the current campus ideologist.

The point is that criminals may be denied the opportunities for such attitudinal elaboration. Society consistently attributes to sex offenders, for example, a set of wholly irrational motives: 'Something must have come over him', 'he didn't know what he was doing'.[6] In other words we deny them an ideology, insisting that their behaviour is initiated and sustained by sudden psychic impulses or aberrations, rather than proceeding from a self-conscious view of what is desirable in sexual behaviour. Similarly we do not attribute to violent offenders the degree of sophistication in motives that we allow to political revolutionaries who use violence.

The self-programming of our course in E-Wing coupled with our commitment towards appreciating 'the ordinary subject's philosophical definition of his general predicament' led us towards creating a climate in which the men were above all *allowed* to have ideologies. Further, we provided – sometimes simply by drawing their attention to certain books – those ideologies which enabled them to retain their 'normality' although they have been or were engaged in behaviour which might commonly be viewed as extremely abnormal. In this respect we might have helped them in rationalizing their behaviour, not in the sense of providing them with excuses or letting them off any moral hooks, but in restoring a rational and intellectual interpretative framework to what they had done.

We talk of 'restoring' only in a very loose sense; it would be

6. Laurie Taylor, 'The Significance and Interpretation of Motivational Accounts', *Sociology*, (January 1972).

romantic to pretend that many of the men ever *had* a well-articulated ideology grounded in respectable philosophical positions. But they did know what they were doing and intended to do what they did. We have given them the chance to identify with others who knew what they were doing and had written about their intentions and justifications. Not that such identifications were always accepted. There was little sympathy with the contemporary hippie forms of drop-out, though some with earlier bohemian movements. Identifications with black radicals in American prisons did not come too easily, but there were some affinities found with political prisoners from a different era, like Victor Serge. And they saw the mildly surrealistic features of some of their own exploits, mirrored in the life styles and manifestoes of the surrealist and Dada movements. While interested in Laing, they could not go all the way with his radical erosion of the boundaries between sick and healthy; they needed to have others defined as clearly pathological.

We do not want to imply that the whole process has been as self-conscious as this discussion suggests. We are still unsure of the extent to which it went on. And it is certainly not unilateral, for we are obviously also in the market for ideologies to sustain aspects of our behaviour and we find ourselves using the research and classes to obtain them. It is not so much that the men have taught us techniques of survival, or that they have 'converted' us, but that our continued awareness of their presence has given us a relativistic, even ironic, perspective on our own psychological survival and our own sustaining ideologies.

They have affected us in many other ways. We would often walk out of the prison gates after an intense discussion with the men and have to spend an evening in an academic or social conversation which seemed, despite the presence of familiar people and objects, more unreal than the world we had just left. Over the years, as we pass through different periods in our lives, we are highly conscious of the men's continuing situation. As we send them picture postcards of our holidays, accounts of concerts, news of friends, we wonder how such fragments are received within the wings, about how they are related by the men to the individuals they knew during the period of the research. For these men, as we have observed elsewhere, know more about our obsessions and anxieties than most other people: When we move our homes, or change our jobs, their letters have a habit of undermining our newly manifested sense of purpose by recalling our old cynicisms; they cast doubt upon the reality of our new romances by recalling our earlier fervours. Unlike our present friends they do not know our new rationalizations well enough to condone our apparent inconsistencies. They compare the relative simplicity of their world with the cultural hustle of our own, hope that we are well and apologize for taking up our time with their letters.

Beyond Reform

We have only described four years in the lives of men who are facing up to five times that number of years inside. For others, being sentenced every week now in our courts, the process will be repeated, the problems of psychological survival will be the same. But is there no hope of change? Can the system not be reformed in such a way that our analysis will be of interest only to future historians of the penal system? We will briefly survey the prospects for reform, but let us cheat by anticipating our conclusion: namely, that we see no evidence for the emergence of any alternative policy to the containment of an increasing number of criminals in conditions like those we have described.

We have reviewed every official policy document, every ministerial statement, every piece of relevant research and find no signs of change in them. Less predictably, penal reform bodies such as the Howard League for Penal Reform and Radical Alternatives to Prison give little indication of where major changes might occur. We can find no statement that does not recognize two 'facts': firstly, the existence of a small group of men who have to be given long sentences and have to

187

be kept under conditions of maximum security and, secondly, the certainty that the numbers in this group will continue to increase. Within the circumference of these assumptions, there is room for manoeuvre, but not very much.

The simple starting-off point is that in the absence of the death penalty, transportation or deliberate physical torture, the only way our society can think of dealing with certain offenders is to send them to prison for very long periods. The identity of this group is firmly established in the rhetoric of crime control: they are menaces to society, evil, depraved, dangerous. Conceptions of evil are not publicly acceptable in contemporary liberal penology and so one finds the attributes of this group referred to almost embarrassingly, as if one is too squeamish to acknowledge their existence. Thus as a 1965 Government White Paper[7] reluctantly admitted:

The first need is to protect society against the dangerous man or woman who by crime will disturb its peace if at large. The idea that anybody is incurably wicked is distasteful and hard to accept. But experience shows there are some who just will not make friends with society ever. Against them society must be protected, not revenged. It does none of us any good to enjoy a sense of revenge. Such evil-doers must be kept apart, for long periods; in the exceptional case, even for life, though such a decision would only be reached, and then with the greatest reluctance, where the protection of the public rendered it clearly essential.

Behind such phrases there is some disagreement about the exact nature of this group and we recognize the possibility that – given certain social and political changes – its range can be either narrowed or widened. Widening is the more likely alternative in the current climate. The categorization policy introduced by the Mountbatten Report formalized certain boundaries. The one per cent of convicted adult male prisoners who made up Category A were all supposed to be those whose escape would be highly dangerous to the police, the public or

7. *The Adult Offender*, (HMSO, December 1965, Cmnd. 2852).

the security of the State. Almost all are serving sentences of 10 years or longer, forty per cent life. The selection for this category is not without problems and much energy is currently expended in the Prison Department in deciding which men fit the criteria and which should be downgraded or recategorized. Besides, prisoners who are escape risks, and prisoners who are serving long sentences are not necessarily the same group. The key Radzinowicz Report recognized that 'the concepts of "maximum security" prisoners and "dangerous" prisoners are certainly difficult and shifting ones'[8] and devoted much discussion to the question of which prisoners need maximum security. Clearly then, there is some slight room for flexibility in future years in deciding who should be subjected to particular régimes.

There is also some room for manoeuvre in deciding whether these prisoners will all be contained in one setting or whether they will be mixed up with others. A dominant part of the debate about long-term and high-risk prisoners has consisted of the conflict between two policies: *concentration* and *dispersal*. The first term (whose somewhat unfortunate historical connotations do not seem to have disturbed many) refers to the policy of creating a single, purpose-built prison, to contain the most dangerous and notorious prisoners of the system. The models of Alcatraz and Devil's Island are the most frequently mentioned and the siting of the prison on the Ise of Wight was proposed. The alternative solution encompassed in the term dispersal is more ambiguous: it ranges from suggestions to disperse the dangerous prisoners more or less randomly through the system, locking them in groups of ten to twenty in special security wings within about half a dozen ordinary prisons and finally, mixing them with other medium- to short-termers and locking them in a number of purpose-built high security prisons, each containing about 400 men.

The Home Office opted for dispersal. The Radzinowicz

8. Home Office, 'The Régime for Long-Term Prisoners in Conditions of Maximum Security', (*Report of the Advisory Council on the Penal System*, HMSO, 1968), p. 10.

Report noted that although concentration would make it easier to provide 'near absolute security', the atmosphere in an institution populated only by evil and dangerous men, might become repressive and the maintenance of good order would be difficult. Instead, Category A prisoners should be dispersed in a number of long-term prisons whose security would be strengthened. They would be mixed in these prisons with a number of Category B prisoners, resulting in units of 300–400 prisoners. A small 'segregation unit' (the current euphemism for punishment block) is to form part of each of these dispersal prisons. This policy is now slowly being implemented, not without opposition – for example, from the Prison Officers' Association who are in favour of concentration and the complete segregation of 'the weak from the bad and the bad from the dangerous'. Whichever form of segregation is advocated, it is informed by a concern to find the best way to control difficult men and this inevitably cuts down any flexibility in the system.

Sheldon Messinger, in his study of what he terms the 'strategies of control' developed in the California prison system over the last fifteen years, describes this management by segregation.[9] Potential or actual troublemakers ('security risks') are concentrated in one place to protect other institutions and in the hope that some means may be found for dealing with them collectively. The strategy is fairly simple: 'identify potential troublemakers as early as possible, try to bring them to heel, if you fail, segregate them'. Given that the organization's prime objective is control, officials find that other strategies don't work: force can only be used occasionally (in riots and demonstrations) and cannot make inmates positively want to do things; motivation through punishment or reward is limited; officials cannot freely choose the prison population. So the control issue – which dominates the daily routine for all levels of prison officials – resolves itself into either motivating prisoners to do what the management wants or neutralizing

9. Sheldon Messinger, *Strategies of Control*, (Center for the Study of Law and Society, University of California, Berkeley, 1969) especially chapters three and five.

the recalcitrants. With restrictions on the legitimate use of force, the strategy of segregation becomes the only answer.

In California this has been achieved both by concentrating the high risks in one prison and creating separate units within prisons such as adjustment centres and segregation units. This strategy leads to an elaboration of various levels of deprivation, supervision and restriction: there are 'honour units' and 'non-honour units', temporary isolation cells, adjustment centres for more permanent segregation and even 'indeterminate' segregation units.

Messinger describes how one adjustment centre in which disruptive inmates were segregated (on very similar lines to the British security wings), eventually spawned its own segregation unit to deal with those prisoners it could not control. The 'complicated Chinese box effect' which resulted 'with inmates in the innermost box ideally required to traverse each enclosing one on the way to relative freedom' is, we believe, precisely the way the English penal system is evolving. Whether or not the strategy of segregation works in minimizing disruption, there is little reason to suppose that the Prison Department of the Home Office will devise any other solution in the coming years.

While concentration versus dispersal may provide a slight variation in the methods of managing long-term prisoners, not even this amount of flexibility is likely to be found in the courts, where judges continue to impose very long sentences. There is no indication that the upward trend in sentencing we recorded in Chapter One shows any sign of tailing off. We expect longer prison sentences will be given out to more offenders and that the pressure for a life sentence to mean just that will become more strident and respectable.[10] Such sentences make nonsense of the belief that their aims are anything but

10. In September 1971 a Conservative M.P., Mr Geoffrey Archer, was most insistent in pressing the Home Secretary to disclose how many lifers had actually died in prison. The infrequency of such events obviously reflected badly on the Home Office who, he implied, were trying to hide this dereliction of duty from the public.

PSYCHOLOGICAL SURVIVAL

deterrent, denunciatory and protective. They are ways of pro-
tecting society by keeping offenders out of circulation as long
as possible. The men are seen as recalcitrants and incorrigibles,
and therefore, beyond reform. Such sentiments as those enshrined in Rule 1 of the 1964 Prison Rules 'the purpose of
training and treatment . . . shall be to establish in them the
will to lead a good and useful life on discharge and fit them to
do so' – had a hollow ring in the corridors of E-Wing. The
pretence of training and treatment is for the most part not even
maintained. It is hardly surprising to find even such progressive figures as ex-con turned penal reformer, Frank Norman
writing:

When in February 1967 the suggestion was made that various
long-term prisoners like the train-robbers should be quietly
eliminated, this bizarre reflection gained enthusiastic support
from some sections of society. But perhaps it is a more realistic
solution than incarcerating men in granite tombs for years on
end.[11]

The penal system as a whole is caught up in the dilemma
pointed to by John Conrad: 'Though change is given verbal
primacy by those who manage the correctional apparatus, their
subordinates are absorbed in the issues of control.'[12]

Such an analysis is even more applicable in the case of long-
term, maximum security prisons. Sykes's comments about the
staff attitude of the New Jersey prison he studied are echoed
by the Morrises in their study of Pentonville and in all other
relevant research:

Officials of the prison, then, are indifferent to the task of reform, not in the sense that they reject reform out of hand as a
legitimate organizational objective, but in the sense that rehabilitation tends to be seen as a theoretical, distant, and somewhat
irrelevant by-product of successful performance at the tasks of

11. Frank Norman, *Lock 'Em Up and Count 'Em*, (London: Charles
Knight, 1970), p. 6.
12. John Conrad, *Crime and Its Correction*, (London, Tavistock,
1965), p. 15.

custody and internal order. A released prisoner may or may not commit another crime in the free community, but that crude test of the prison's accomplishments in the area of reform lies far away. Within the walls, in the clear-cut scope of the custodian's responsibilities, the occurrence of escapes and disorders is a weightier concern.[13]

Despite this, we are assured by the Home Office that the emphasis on security and containment is not antithetical to change:

Another criticism of present policies is also heard. It is that emphasis on security . . . must hamper the longer-term prevention of crime by making more difficult the task of rehabilitation . . . But the simple antithesis of security versus rehabilitation is false. One does not vary in inverse proportion to the other.[14]

In this last notion – a relaxed régime within conditions of maximum perimeter security – lies the real alternative to pure incarceration. The alternative is *not* rehabilitation, training or treatment, nor we believe, can it ever be in the present ideological climate; the alternative is, in the words of the same Home Office document 'humane containment'. The new ideology is that of liberal penal management and its adherents see as the only obstacles to its implementation such technical factors as inadequate staff training, lack of financial resources and out of date buildings. To quote a benign version of the ideology stated in the Mountbatten Report:

The principal reason why these prisons are not secure today is that solitary confinement for long periods of years is no longer tolerable to the public conscience. Prisoners are allowed out of their cells and are permitted to talk to their fellow prisoners. They work at various trades. They are allowed periods of recreation together. These reforms have been introduced over many decades by successive governments. Prison governors are now expected to treat the prisoners in their charge with humanity and to do their best to devise a régime which will prepare them for

13. Gresham Sykes, *The Society of Captives*, p. 38.
14. *People in Prisons*, (HMSO, 1969, Cmnd. 4214, p. 8).

living an honest life at the end of their sentence but at the same time they are expected to prevent them from escaping. A constructive liberal prison régime and secure prisons are not necessarily incompatible, but conflicts will arise if an attempt is made to conduct a liberal régime in buildings designed in accordance with the 19th century philosophy of prison treatment. Treating prisoners by modern methods in out of date buildings inevitably means that some of them can escape.[15]

We do not wish to scoff at such alternatives and where they have been spelt out in detail, they recognize the very problems that we have pointed to in our own analysis. Thus the recommendations in the Radzinowicz Report on the long-term imprisonment in maximum security show a highly sensitive awareness of the qualities lacking in the present system: the need to preserve self-respect, to give the prisoner some choice and autonomy, to allow him variety and some movement, to give him privacy.

We believe, however, that the ideology of liberal penal management is limited in ways that render it virtually bankrupt as an alternative policy.

In the first place even the most minimal humane or liberal changes are simply not being implemented in the way the public have been assured they will be. In 1966 the Mountbatten Committee made its often quoted indictment of conditions in the wings being 'as such no country with a record for civilized behaviour ought to tolerate any longer than is absolutely necessary as a stop-gap measure'.[16] Two years later in 1968, the Advisory Council on the Penal System noted that although improvements in the wings had been made 'no one regards the containment of prisoners in such small confined units as anything other than a temporary and most undesirable expedient'.[17] A year later – in the November 1969 publication,

15. *The Régime for Long-Term Prisoners*, p. 53.
16. *Report of the Inquiry into Prison Escapes and Security*, (HMSO, 1966, Cmnd. 3175).
17. *Report of the Advisory Council on the Penal System*, (HMSO, 1968).

People in Prisons – we were assured that: 'Conditions in these wings, and the adjacent exercise areas, have been much improved since they were opened, but it remains undesirable that men should be detained for very long periods in such confined conditions.'[18]

As we write this chapter in the spring of 1972 Durham's E-Wing no longer exists, but there are at least three other prisons duplicating similar conditions.

But even if some of these changes were to be implemented and the resistance to them by the ordinary prison staff overcome, they can hardly alter the fundamental nature of long-term imprisonment. The experience is meant to be punitive and depriving, the confinement is meant to be total. The régime might turn out to be relaxed, permissive, liberal or humane and the prisoner's suffering might be an object of genuine concern rather than indifference, but the aims of coercion and custody must remain dominant.

It is interesting to reflect at this period in penal history when the judiciary has opted for longer and longer sentences that we have no way of assessing the meaning of deprivation of liberty. Alone amongst criminologists Nils Christie has attempted to discuss the way in which the price of liberty changes over time, pointing out that loss of liberty in our contemporary society which lauds freedom and individualism may well be more psychically costly than in those societies where ideas of liberty and individual freedom are not so well developed.[19] In other words we may be increasing sentences at that particular period in history when the pains involved in loss of liberty are already at a premium.

Finally, to remain faithful to our theoretical perspective we must see how all this looks from the point of view of the prisoners themselves. We have said enough about their problems to conclude that simple changes in the régime can hardly be

18. *People in Prisons. England and Wales*, (HMSO, 1969, Cmnd. 4214).

19. Nils Christie, 'Changes in Penal Values' in *Scandinavian Studies in Criminology* (London, Tavistock, 1968, vol. II).

expected to make much difference to their environment. They very much welcome things which to the outsider seem minor concessions or changes and they are pleasantly surprised to be transferred to an environment which turns out better than expected. Thus Jock wrote to us from Leicester, a wing with a very bad reputation:

As you see from the above, I'm now back once more at the 'Inferno'. However, I must be honest and say that there has been a marked improvement since my previous stay here . . . The chokey cells which were once full here are now practically empty. This is always a good sign, I think.

He went on to talk about the more humane visiting conditions, the new furniture, the cookery classes and the important concession of extra P.T. David, transferred at the same time to Leicester, also noted that: 'the racks, hot irons and thumb screws are to some extent the product of over-active imaginations. Treasonous as it may sound, I prefer it here to Durham . . . There is a very noticeable difference in the staff; it's refreshing after the poisonous atmosphere and mutual snarlings at Durham.'

But the men are all too aware that such concessions and changes hardly touch the basic problems; moreover, the initial satisfaction with change has a way – as it does in the outside world – of turning sour soon enough. Thus Roy, who wrote in glowing terms about the régime two weeks after his transfer to Chelmsford, six weeks later wrote in altogether more despairing tones: 'Sorry to report a deflation of my optimistic bubble. The community of optimism transferred out and my old community from Durham transferred in, with all of its attendant baggage of problems immediately recreating the atmosphere that I had hoped I'd left behind.'

The men are continually contradicting themselves and each other about what sort of régime they would like: a small wing or a large wing, concentration or dispersal, more work or less work, a soft governor or an old fashioned governor. Such contradictions confirm for them Baudelaire's lines: 'life is a hospital, in which every patient is possessed by the desire to change his bed. This one would prefer to suffer in front of the stove, and that one believes he would get well if he were placed by the window.' [20] Only for them, this is not an indulgent literary metaphor, but the real thing. And for this reason, humane containment and liberal penal management has very little to offer them.

Do You Think That I'll Be Different?

In his *Ballad of San Quentin* Johnny Cash sings about the prison:

What good do you think you do?
Do you think that I'll be different when I'm through?

The question of whether the experience of long-term imprisonment does any 'good', is, as we've argued, more or less irrelevant. From the point of view of the prison authorities, liberal penal management might be ideologically, politically and perhaps even practically, a good solution, but the 'good' it is supposed to be doing is for the society that is being protected rather than for the individual prisoner. Few prisoners see the régime as beneficial, the work as rehabilitative, the experience as valuable.

But whether they'll be different when they're 'through' is another matter. The sporadic liberal concern about the possible deteriorating effects of long sentences is, as we've shown, more than matched by the men's own obsessive anxiety and fear on these grounds. Can one emerge alive – and above all, alive and unchanged? Such questions can only begin to be answered by the official research project on the 'psychological changes associated with long-term imprisonment' (see Appendix). The differences revealed by tests of reaction time, extraversion,

20. Charles Baudelaire, 'Anywhere out of the World' from Joseph Bernstein (ed.) *Baudelaire, Rimbaud, Verlaine*, (New York, Citadel Press, 1947), p. 163.

attitudes to authority are too superficial to do justice to the complexity of any changes. We take it for granted that even mild dislocations of our ordinary life will produce changes more significant than these. We talk of a few years on a new job mellowing somebody or a few years of marriage as making someone else a changed person.

How can we begin to assess the differences that might result from long years of imprisonment? After four or five years' study of the problem we are only in the position to provide the limited answers contained in this book. For example, we have described how contacts with the outside world become more difficult to sustain and differences from this world become more manifest; how men with no workable sustaining ideologies retreat or else fight in self-destructive ways; how problems of day-to-day management become easier to cope with in an unreflexive way, but also how the ultimate existential problem, the fear of deterioration, becomes more and more acute.

Few of these changes will be adaptive to the outside world which some of the men will eventually enter. There is much attention in ordinary prisons to preparing the inmate for this transition: vocational training, half-way hostels, pre-release programmes. In one review of such measures [21] the programmes which try to cushion the impact of the inmate's transition between incarceration and community living are compared to those used with tunnel workers who do day-long construction in caissons far underground. These workers ('sandhogs') must be readjusted in a decompression chamber if they are to cope with normal air conditions at ground level, otherwise they might suffer the 'bends'.

We do not know whether the Home Office envisages such programmes for long-term prisoners. Certainly those provided now for ordinary prisoners do not inspire much confidence and if a mere adaptation of them to long-termers is planned, they can hardly deal with the social and psychological 'bends' the

21. 'Graduated Release' in *Monograph Series of National Institute of Mental Health*, (US Govt., Washington, 1971).

men will face as they re-surface. It is not much use training them in work skills and habits which will be out of date when they leave or – as is the case in one pre-release programme – giving them 'tips for the wardrobe'.

The men themselves do not spend much time discussing what they will do when released. For most of them such thoughts provoke too much anxiety or else are simply unrealistic at this stage of their sentences. In his study of convicts in San Quentin John Irwin found that 'looking outside' was a major preoccupation. The men would discuss and fantasize various styles of 'making it' (staying out of prison) and 'doing all right': how to catch up on immediate gratification missed while inside and to fulfil long-term goals and desires. These styles involved such themes as abundant sexual possibilities, relative financial comfort, excitement, sharpness and autonomy. Their variants included conventional ones (the playboy, the rich old lady); marginal (bohemian, expatriate, revolutionary) and criminal (the 'one big score' plan, the escapade). It is probable that as the men we knew approach their release date, such fantasies and styles will become more apparent: at the moment, they are too remote to be contemplated without arousing despair.

This brings us back to one of the themes of this book: the concern with the everyday, mundane features of our social environment. A criticism that has often been levelled at our account of prison survival is that it is too heavy; it reads too much into the situation; it makes the simple look complicated. The point though, is that a self-conscious account of how people cope with any situation – family, work, school – would generate much the same sort of questions. Neither the self-consciousness of our analysis nor the self-consciousness we attribute to the men, implies that they spend every minute of the day reflecting on their predicament. The same extreme situation which created their problems of survival is benign enough to eventually offer solutions which become just part of day-to-day life. They become routine and taken for granted – as they do outside.

But we don't want to end on a note which sounds suspiciously like an assertion that the prison is, after all, just a microcosm of society. It has already become a literary cliché to use prisons, leper colonies, T.B. sanatoria, cancer wards or mental hospitals in this way. But our descriptions are not meant to be symbolic, analogical, metaphorical or allegorical: this would be to do violence to a phenomenon whose reality we have tried – incompletely – to convey.

Appendix

The story of another research project

As this book is not primarily addressed to those interested in the niceties of the social scientific method, we felt that the text was not the place in which to embark on a detailed criticism of the methodology used in other prison research. But we are faced with the somewhat unusual coincidence that a piece of research exists which appears to duplicate ours exactly: it concerned the same problems – the effects of long-term imprisonment. It was carried out in similar settings, over roughly the same period and even using some of our sample. As this research will inevitably compete with ours for official and public attention, we thought it important to give it some consideration. The critical summary of it in this Appendix should not be read, though, as an invidious singling out of one project: such research is fairly representative of the psychological studies of prison populations which command official credibility.[1]

In the 1969 Home Office publication *People in Prisons* the following was listed under the heading 'Research Supported by Home Office Grant':

Durham University 'An investigation of psychological changes associated with long-term imprisonment.'

1. For evidence on this, readers are directed to the following sources: *British Journal of Social and Clinical Psychology*; *British Journal of Criminology*; *Exerpta Criminologica*; *Crime and Delinquency Abstracts*; various publications of the Council of Europe's Committee on Crime Problems and regular lists issued by the Home Office of research supported or funded.

More details – the first in public as far as we know – were provided two years later in an obscure publication of the Council of Europe.[2] From these and other sources, we know that the starting date of the project was 1968 and its expected date of completion 1972. The Home Office is sponsoring the project with an initial grant of £16,000. A final report on the research is due in October 1972. To date, some interim reports (mainly on methodology) have been sent to the Home Office and an article will be published in a psychological journal subject to Home Office veto under the Official Secrets Act.

The design of the research is roughly as follows. A sample of about 200 prisoners serving determinate sentences of 10 years or life imprisonment was initially tested. Some seventy of the prisoners were in Wakefield, forty in Blundeston (a prison specializing in the rehabilitation of 'inadequate' offenders) and about twenty each from Parkhurst and Dartmoor. There were only two or three men from Durham. Some attempt was made to include different types of offenders and the sample covered predominately Category B men. Some thirty prisoners (fifteen per cent) refused to be 'tested', a proportion that the researchers considered to be fairly low. These were 'replaced' in the sample by more cooperative prisoners. (Apparently a snowballing effect operated whereby one prisoner who refused to take part would persuade his friends to take the same line.) When the researchers arrived in Durham, they were met by a partial boycott: one member of our class was apparently delegated to inform them as politely as possible that their research approach did not meet the approval of most of their subjects, and would they please try some other prisoners – which they did.[3]

---

2. *International Exchange of Information on Current Criminological Research Projects in Member States*, Number 11, European Committee on Crime Problems, Council of Europe, (Strasbourg 1971), pp. 61–2.

3. Prisoners have many irritations with which to cope as we have indicated elsewhere. It appears that in addition to these, they are also harassed by researchers.

To ensure a 'cross-sectional comparison' – that is, to have prisoners at different stages of their sentences – the sample was divided into four equal groups (i) new inmates; (ii) prisoners having served three years; (iii) prisoners having served five years and (iv) prisoners having served seven years. In order to make a 'longitudinal comparison' – that is, to see changes over time – it was intended to follow up each group at the end of the study. In the event, only fifteen months elapsed between the initial and final tests. Two other comparisons were written into the design: men who left prison (on ordinary discharges or parole) were compared with those who remained, in order to see which changes were attributable to being in prison and which due to the passage of time. Similarly a control group was constructed and tested over the equivalent time periods to see which changes would have occurred naturally among men of similar age in the non-prison population. Some difficulty was encountered in finding reasonable controls and the final sample contained a mixture of various groups including some from the Territorial Army.

The tests themselves fell into four groups. The first was cognitive and intellectual (I.Q. and similar measurements) and was to be used to answer the question about possible deterioration of the men's intellectual abilities. The second group measured reaction time: speed in responding to flashing lights and other stimuli. The third group involved tests of personality and included the Eysenck Personality Inventory and items compiled from other standard scales. The fourth area was attitudinal and used devices such as the semantic differential to establish attitudes to such concepts as 'authority', 'law' and 'police'.

As the first results came through, the major finding was simply that there were no significant differences at all, on any of the dimensions, between men who had served different periods in prison (that is, on the cross-sectional analysis). This made the researchers change their tactics altogether: they abandoned the 1–3–5–7 year comparisons and calculated from prison records the *overall* time that each member of the sample had spent in prison. Now, contrasting long- and short-timers, some differences were indeed found.

The two groups did not differ significantly as far as intelligence was concerned, but the long-termers were more introvert, more hostile to authority and in some cases had poorer scores on tests of reaction time and motor skills. Of course, what is being measured here are not *changes* but *differences*. The long-termers may have been more introvert, more hostile to authority and less skilled than the short-termers when they first arrived in prison. These figures can – by concentrating on differences and not processes – only suggest actual changes.

Leaving this particular project aside – for our knowledge of its findings is only preliminary and it might possibly take another direction in its last stages – we can only point out that the sort of results that can be obtained using such methods must be limited. 'Limited' in the sense that they cannot fully comprehend the effects of long-term imprisonment by relying upon the examination of such a narrow range of dimensions, by ignoring the meaning of the situation in which the tests were given, and by using such a short time period between test and retest. A longitudinal study which only looks at changes over fifteen months, when long-termers are increasingly serving sentences of over 10 years is necessarily somewhat circumscribed. The finding that long-termers are more negative to authority and more introvert than short-termers is not on the face of it particularly surprising. The reference to introversion implies a deep personality characteristic, but one must remember that 'extravert' and 'introvert' are short-hand words for summarizing a group of responses to a questionnaire and that this questionnaire is designed to measure the attitudes of individuals whose relationship to a world of behavioural possibilities sets them completely apart from the long-term prisoner. Consider, for example, the character of the extravert; as depicted by his most authoritative portrayer, H. J. Eysenck:

He is more likely to change his work, his profession, move from one company to another, or change departments within one company. He is more liable to change house, to move from one part of the town to another, or even from one city to somewhere else. He is more likely to change his food preferences from day to day, or even his clothes. He is more likely to change girl friends, or at a later stage, to get divorced and change wives. He is less likely to stick to one and the same car for a long period of time, or to the same colour scheme in his house, or even to the same furniture.[4]

It is not altogether surprising that a scale designed to measure the presence of such extravert characteristics finds less evidence of their existence amongst prisoners who have faced years inside. But such scores have undoubted scientific interest to experimental psychologists.

It is important to understand that a principal function of official research into crime and punishment is to reassure the public that the problem is being scientifically tackled. The research itself may or may not say anything significant, relevant or even interesting. Its results indeed may never get published. This is relatively unimportant. The main thing is the research's WDP (window dressing potential). To have a high WDP the research must fulfil the following criteria: it must be well financed; it must be comprehensible to most politicians and administrators; its aims must be presented in a simple direct way, preferably in the form of a hypothesis to be tested. Any complex theoretical and methodological problems must be kept to one side and the results, when they appear, should be ambiguous enough to reassure, while at the same time generating numerous statements of the 'more research is needed' variety.

Current research on the effects of long-term imprisonment scores fairly well on all these criteria and followed a familiar three-stage chronology:

i) *A problem emerges or is created, it is defined in simplistic terms and comments of the 'we don't know enough about it' type appear in editorials and political speeches.*

4. H. J. Eysenck, *Fact and Fiction in Psychology*, (Penguin, 1968), p. 81.

In the period leading to the mid-sixties with the end of the death penalty in sight and with the increase in the use of very long prison sentences some anxiety was felt about the effects of long-term sentences. Were they a genuine deterrent? Did they have a (perhaps permanent) disintegrating effect on the offender and, in this sense, was not the death penalty a 'kinder' punishment? What about security considerations: how many restrictions could a person live under for long periods? Such questions were translated into official problems in numerous concerned and official quarters,[5] the most crucial of which was the influential Radzinowicz Report (1968) which noted:

Practically nothing is known about the vital subject of the lasting effects on human personality of long-term imprisonment, yet pronouncements on the subject continue to be made and very long prison sentences continue to be imposed.[6]

There were many other references in the report to the need for research on deterioration defined, as elsewhere, almost exclusively in terms of cognitive and intellectual skills.

ii) *A hastily designed piece of research is commissioned by the appropriate body or emanates from the academic community.*

At the beginning of 1966 security and long-term imprisonment became big stories as well as objects of official concern with the events we described in Chapter One. These events were, of course, even bigger news locally, and at times like these, the local press, radio and television invariably contact the university experts on such matters. Projects – of the sort we have described in this Appendix – are often stimulated in this way. The Home Office then accepts them with a speed

5. For some examples see the Home Office White Paper *The Adult Offender*, (Cmnd. 2852, December 1965), p. 3; a Young Fabian Pamphlet, *The Adult Criminal*, (February 1967, p. 3) and an article by Hugh Klare, Secretary of the Howard League for Penal Reform, 'Prisons Since the Mountbatten Report', *New Society* (31 August 1967, p. 287).

6. *The Régime for Long-Term Prisoners in Conditions of Maximum Security*, (HMSO 1968), p. 71.

and enthusiasm best understandable in terms of the current demands of penal policy.

iii) *The public is then ritualistically reassured that things are in control.*

This final stage has not yet been reached, but we predict that – irrespective of the good intentions of the researchers or the rigour with which they have applied their approved methodology – the results of projects such as we have described will be used to provide reassurance about the nature of long-term imprisonment. They will do little to disturb the political and legal structure, although they should provide some hollow laughs among that most obsessive and compulsive group of consumers of government reports on prison life – the long-termers in British prisons.

Selected Bibliography

The following books and articles have been useful to us during our research, although not all have been referred to explicitly in the text.

Research Methods

BECKER, Howard, *Sociological Work*, Allen Lane The Penguin Press, 1971.

CICOUREL, A. V., *Method and Measurement in Sociology*, New York, Free Press, 1964.

FICHTER, J. H. and KOLB, W. L., 'Ethical Limitations on Sociological Reporting', *American Sociological Review*, 18 October 1953.

FRIEDMAN, Neil, *The Social Nature of Psychological Research*, New York, Basic Books, 1967.

MATZA, David, *Becoming Deviant*, Englewood Cliffs, Prentice Hall, 1969.

ORNE, Martin T., 'On the Social Psychology of the Psychological Experiment' in P. G. Swingle (ed.) *Experiments in Social Psychology*, New York, Academic Press, 1968.

ROSENTHAL, Robert, *Experimenter Effects in Behavioral Research*, New York, Appleton Century Crofts, 1960.

ROSENTHAL, R. and ROSNOW, R. (eds), *Sources of Artefact in Social Research*, New York, Academic Press, 1970.

TOCH, Hans, 'The Convict as Researcher' in I. L. Horowitz and M. S. Strong (eds) *Sociological Realities*, New York, Harper & Row, 1971.

Extreme Situations

1. Psychological Studies of Stress and Deprivation

HERON, W., BEXTON, W. H., and HEBB, D. O., 'Cognitive effects of a decreased variation to the sensory environment', *The American Psychologist*, 8, 1953.

SELECTED BIBLIOGRAPHY

MCGRATH, Joseph E. (ed.), *Social and Psychological Factors in Stress*, New York, Holt, Rinehart & Winston, 1970.

ORNE, M. T. and SCHEIBE, K. E., 'The Contribution of Non-privation Factors in the Production of Sensory Deprivation Effects: The Psychology of the "Panic Button"', *Journal of Abnormal and Social Psychology*, 68, 1964.

PROSHANSKY, H. M., ITTELSON, W. H., and RIVLIN, L. G. (eds), *Environmental Psychology*, New York, Holt, Rinehart & Winston, 1970 (esp. article by John Lilly 'Mental Effects of Reduction of Ordinary Levels of Physical Stimuli on Intact Healthy Persons').

VERNON, Jack, *Inside the Black Room: Studies in Sensory Deprivation*, Penguin, 1965.

SOLOMON, P. et. al., *Sensory Deprivation: A Symposium*, Cambridge, Harvard University Press, 1961.

2. Exploration and Discovery

ANDERSON, J. R. L., *The Ulysses Factor: The Exploring Instinct in Man*, London, Hodder & Stoughton, 1970.

BYRD, Richard E., *Alone*, London, Putnam, 1938.

CHERRY-GARRARD, A., *The Worst Journey in the World*, Penguin, 1970.

CHICHESTER, Francis, *Alone Across the Atlantic*, London, Hodder & Stoughton, 1961.

HERZOG, Maurice, *Annapurna*, London, Cape, 1952.

KNOX-JOHNSTON, Robin, *A World of My Own*, London, Cassell, 1969.

MERRIEN, J., *Lonely Voyagers*, New York, G. P. Putnam & Sons, 1954.

NAYLOR, Merton, *Penance Way*, London, Hutchinson, 1968.

SCOTT, R. F., *Scott's Last Expedition*, London, John Murray, 1927.

SLOCUM, Joshua, *Sailing Alone Around the World*, London, Hart-Davis, 1948.

3. Migration and Disaster

BAKER, George W., and CHAPMAN, Dwight W., *Man and Society in Disaster*, New York, Basic Books, 1962.

BARTON, Alan H. et al., *Social Organization Under Stress: A Sociological Review of Disaster Studies*, Washington D.C., National Academy of Sciences, 1963.

BRODY, E. B. (ed.), *Behavior in New Environments*, New York, Sage Publications, 1969.

BURNS, N. M., CHAMBERS, R. H. and HENDLER, E. (eds), *Unusual Environments and Human Behavior*, New York, Free Press, 1963.

DESMOND, Cosmas, *The Discarded People*, Penguin, 1971 (foreword by Nadine Gordimer).

FRITZ, Charles E., 'Disaster', in R. K. Merton and R. A. Nisbet (eds), *Contemporary Social Problems*, London, Hart-Davis, 1963.

KILLIAN, Louis, 'The Significance of Multiple Group Membership in Disaster', *American Journal of Sociology*, LVII, 1952, pp. 309–14.

THOMAS, W. L. and ZNANIECKI, F., *The Polish Peasant in Europe and America*, 2nd edn, 2 vols, New York, Dover, 1958.

WALLACE, A. F., *Human Behavior in Extreme Situations*, Washington D.C., National Academy of Sciences, 1956.

Friendship and Privacy

HEIDER, F., *The Psychology of Interpersonal Relations*, New York, John Wiley, 1958.

NEWCOMB, T. M., *The Acquaintance Process*, New York, Holt, Rinehart and Winston, 1961.

SCHACHTER, S., *The Psychology of Affiliation: Experimental Studies of the Sources of Gregariousness*, Stanford Calif.; Stanford University Press, 1959.

WESTIN, Alan, *Privacy and Freedom*, London, Bodley Head, 1970.

Institutionalization, Deterioration, Self Identity

BARTON, Russell, *Institutional Neurosis*, 2nd edn, Bristol, John Wright, 1966.

SELECTED BIBLIOGRAPHY

BETTELHEIM, Bruno, 'Individual and Mass Behavior in Extreme Situations', *Journal of Abnormal and Social Psychology*, XXXVIII (1943, pp. 417–52).

BETTELHEIM, Bruno, *The Informed Heart*, New York, Free Press of Glencoe, 1960.

BLUHM, Hilde O., 'How did They Survive? Mechanisms of Defence in Nazi Concentration Camps', *American Journal of Psychotherapy*, 2 (1948, pp. 3–32).

GOFFMAN, Erving, *Asylums*, Penguin, 1968.

GOFFMAN, Erving, *Stigma*, Penguin, 1968.

GORDON, C. and GERGEN, K. J. (eds), *The Self in Social Interaction*, New York, John Wiley, 1968.

LAING, R. D., *The Divided Self*, Penguin, 1965.

ROSENBERG, Bernard, et. al. (eds), *Mass Society in Crisis*, London, Collier Macmillan, 1964.

STEIN, Maurice, et. al., *Identity and Anxiety: Survival of the Person in Mass Society*, New York, Free Press, 1963.

Ideologies and Life Styles

BERKMAN, Alexander, *Prison Memoirs of an Anarchist*, (originally published 1912), New York, Schocken Books, 1970.

CLEAVER, Eldridge, *Soul on Ice*, London, Cape, 1969.

CLINARD, M. B. and QUINNEY, R., *Criminal Behavior Systems*, New York, Holt, Rinehart & Winston, 1971.

CRESSEY, Donald, *Criminal Organization: Its Elementary Forms*, London, Heinemann, 1972.

DAVIS, Angela Y., *If They Come in the Morning: Voices of Resistance*, London, Orbach & Chambers, 1971.

DE BAUM, Everett, 'The Heist: The Theory and Practice of Armed Robbery', *Harpers Magazine*, February, 1950.

HEPPENSTALL, Rayner, *A Little Pattern of French Crime*, London, Hamish Hamilton, 1969.

HOBSBAWM, E. J., *Bandits*, London, Weidenfeld & Nicolson, 1969; Penguin, 1972.

IRVING, H. B., *Studies of French Criminals of the Nineteenth Century*, London, William Heinemann, 1901.

LONGONI, J. C., *Four Patients of Dr Deibler: A Study in Anarchy*, London, Lawrence and Wishart, 1970.

212

LOUDERBECK, Lew, *Pretty Boy, Baby Face – I Love You*, New York, Fawcett Publications, 1968.

MAILER, Norman, *An American Dream*, London, Mayflower, 1969.

MELL, Ezra Brett, *The Truth About the Bonnot Gang*, London, Coptic Press, 1968 (pamphlet).

PARKER, Tony and ALLERTON, Robert, *The Courage of His Convictions*, London, Hutchinson, 1962.

POLSKY, Ned, *Hustlers, Beats and Others*, Penguin, 1971.

SERGE, Victor, *Memoirs of a Revolutionary*, London, Oxford University Press, 1963.

SUTHERLAND, Edwin, *The Professional Thief*, Chicago, Chicago University Press, 1937.

Time

CALKINS, Kathy, 'Time: Perspectives, Marking and Styles of Usage', *Social Problems*, 17, 4 Spring, 1970.

DAVIS, Fred, 'Definitions of Time and Recovery in Paralytic Polio Convalescence', *American Journal of Sociology* 61 (May 1956, pp. 582–7).

DAVIS, Fred, 'Why All of Us May Be Hippies Someday', *Trans-Action* (5 December 1967).

DOOB, Leonard, *Patterning of Time*, Yale University Press, 1971.

FARBER, Maurice, 'Suffering and Time Perspective in the Prisoner' in Kurt Lewin (ed.), *Studies in Authority and Frustration*, University of Iowa Press, 1944.

FRASER, Ronald, *Work*, Penguin, 1968.

HORTON, John, 'Time and Cool People', *Trans-Action*, 7 April 1967, pp. 5–12.

KASTENBAUM, R., 'Cognitive and Personal Futurity in Later Life', *Journal of Individual Psychology*, 19 (1963, pp. 216–22).

LANDAU, Simha F., 'The Effect of Length of Imprisonment and Subjective Distance from Release on Future Time Perspective and Time Estimation of Prisoners', *Studies in Criminology*, XXI, Jerusalem, Hebrew University.

ORME, John Edward, *Time, Experience and Behavior*, New York, American Elsevier Inc. 1969.

ROTH, Julius, *Timetables*, Indianapolis, Bobbs-Merrill, 1962.

ROY, Donald, ' "Banana Time": Job Satisfaction and Informal Interaction', *Human Organization*, 18, 4 (1959–60, pp. 158–68).

SHAPELEY, H. (ed.), *Time and Its Mysteries*, New York, Collier Books, 1962.

YAKER, Henri et al. (eds), *The Future of Time: Man's Temporal Environment*, New York: Doubleday & Co., 1971.

Prisons: Journalistic Accounts, Sociological Studies

CLAYTON, Tom, *Men in Prison*, London, Hamish Hamilton, 1970.

CLOWARD, Richard et al., *Theoretical Studies in the Social Organization of the Prison*, New York, Social Science Research Council, 1960.

CLEMMER, Donald, *The Prison Community*, (with a foreword by Donald R. Cressey), New York, Holt, Rinehart & Winston, 1961.

CRESSEY, D. R. (ed.), *The Prison: Studies in Institutional Organization and Change*, New York, Holt, Rinehart & Winston, 1961.

CHRISTIANSEN, Karlo, 'Recidivism among Collaborators' in Marvin Wolfgang (ed.), *Crime and Culture*, New York, John Wiley, 1969.

IRWIN, J. and CRESSEY, D., 'Thieves, Convicts and the Inmate Culture', *Social Problems*, (Fall 1962, pp. 152–5).

IRWIN, John, *The Felon*, Englewood Cliffs, N.J., Prentice Hall, 1970.

MATHIESEN, Thomas, *The Defenses of the Weak: A Sociological Study of a Norwegian Correctional Institution*, London, Tavistock, 1965.

MESSINGER, Sheldon, *Strategies of Control*, Unpublished Ms., Center for the Study of Law and Society, University of California, Berkeley, 1969.

MORRIS, Terence and Pauline, *Pentonville: A Sociological Study of an English Prison*, London, Routledge & Kegan Paul, 1963.

PARKER, Tony, *The Frying Pan: A Prison and Its Prisoners*, London, Hutchinson, 1970.

SYKES, Gresham, *The Society of Captives: A Study of a Maximum Security Prison*, Princeton University Press, 1958.

Prisons: Personal Experiences

BEHAN, Brendan, *Borstal Boy*, London, Hutchinson, 1958.

BENNEY, Mark, *Gaol Delivery*, London, Longmans, 1948.

BRUCHAC, Joseph and WITHERUP, William (eds), *Words from the House of the Dead: An Anthology of Prison Writings from Soledad*, Greenfield, New York, Greenfield Review Press, 1971.

BURNEY, Christopher, *Solitary Confinement*, New York, Coward and McCann, 1952.

CARASOV, Victor, *Two Gentlemen to See You, Sir*, London, Gollancz, 1971.

DOSTOYEVSKI, Fyodor, *The House of the Dead*, New York, Random House Edition, 1967.

FIRESTONE, Ross, *Getting Busted: Personal Experiences of Arrest, Trial and Prison*, New York, Douglas Book Corporation, 1970.

GADDIS, Thomas, *Birdman of Alcatraz*, New York, 1956.

GRISWOLD, H. Jack, et al., *An Eye For An Eye*, New York, Pocket Books, 1971.

HARVEY, Richmond, *Prison From Within*, London, Allen & Unwin, 1937.

HASSLER, Alfred, *Diary of a Self Made Convict*, London, Gollancz, 1955.

JACKSON, George, *Soledad Brother: The Prison Letters of George Jackson*, Penguin, 1971.

KNIGHT, Etheridge, *Black Voices from Prison*, New York, Pathfinder Press, 1970.

LEARY, Timothy, *Jail Notes*, New York, Douglas Book Corporation, 1970.

LEOPOLD, Nathan, *Life + 99 Years*, London, Gollancz, 1958.

LEVY, Howard and MILLER, David, *Going to Jail: The Political Prisoner*, New York, Grove Press, 1971.

MARTINSON, Robert, *Social Interaction under Close Confinement*, Institute of Social Sciences, University of California, Berkeley, 1966.

SELECTED BIBLIOGRAPHY

MINTON, Robert (ed.), *Inside: Prison American Style*, New York, Random House, 1971.

MIKES, George (ed.), *Prison: A Symposium*, London, Routledge & Kegan Paul, 1963.

NORMAN, Frank, *Bang to Rights*, London, Secker & Warburg, 1958.

'One Who's There', *County Time*, San Francisco, Connections, no date.

PARKER, Tony, *The Unknown Citizen*, Penguin, 1966.

PELL, Eve (ed.), *Maximum Security: Letters from Prison*, New York, E. P. Dutton & Co., 1972.

SERGE, Victor, *Men in Prison*, London, Gollancz, 1970.

SOLZHENITSYN, Alexander, *One Day in the Life of Ivan Denisovich*, Penguin, 1968.

WILDEBLOOD, Peter, *Against the Law*, Penguin, 1955.

Whisper: A Timescript, London, Whisper Promotions, 1971.

'Zeno', *Life*, London, Pan Books, 1970.

Official Reports and Policy Discussions

HMSO Cmnd. 2068: Report of an Inquiry held by the Visiting Committee into Allegations of Ill Treatment of Prisoners in Her Majesty's Prison, Durham, 1963 (*The Cronkshaw Report*).

HMSO Cmnd. 2296: *The War Against Crime in England and Wales, 1959–64*, 1964.

HMSO Cmnd. 2852: *The Adult Offender*, 1965.

HMSO Cmnd. 3175: Report of the Inquiry into Prison Escapes and Security, 1966 (*The Mountbatten Report*).

HMSO: The Régime for Long-Term Prisoners in Conditions of Maximum Security: Report of the Advisory Council on the Penal System, 1968 (*The Radzinowicz Report*).

HMSO Cmnd. 4214: *People in Prison, England and Wales*, 1969.

HMSO Cmnd. 4708: *Criminal Statistics, England and Wales*, 1970.

HMSO Cmnd. 4724: *Report of the Work of the Prison Department*, 1970.

Young Fabian Pamphlet, *The Adult Criminal*, February 1967.

KLARE, Hugh J., 'Prisons since the Mountbatten Report', *New Society*, vol. 10, no. 257, 31 August 1967.

SELECTED BIBLIOGRAPHY

NORMAN, Frank (ed.), *Lock 'Em Up and Count 'Em: Reform of the Penal System*, London, Charles Knight & Co., 1971.

Radical Alternatives to Prison (R.A.P.): various statements and newsletters available from: 104, Newgate Street, London EC1.

Preservation of the Rights of Prisoners (P.R.O.P.): magazine and statements available from: 96 Victoria Avenue, Hull.

About the Authors

Stanley Cohen completed a degree in sociology and psychology at Witwatersrand University, South Africa, in 1962. He worked in London for a year as a psychiatric social worker and then went to the London School of Economics, where he completed his Ph.D. research on societal reactions to juvenile delinquency. In 1967, after lecturing at Enfield College for two years, he moved as a lecturer in sociology to the University of Durham. Dr Cohen is at present a lecturer at the University of Essex. His publications include various articles on the Teddy Boys, Mods and Rockers, vandalism, political violence and the effects of the mass media on delinquency. He is the author of *Folk Devils and Moral Panics* (1972) and has edited *Images of Deviance* (1971).

Laurie Taylor graduated in psychology from the University of London and went to the University of Leicester where he completed his graduate studies, and has been a lecturer in sociology at the University of York since 1965. Mr Taylor has published many articles on theories of delinquency, alienation, the relationship between psychology and sociology, the social world of the actor and the motivation of sexual offenders. He has also written on the work of Erving Goffman and published a book, *Deviance and Society* (1971). His latest publication (written with R. Robertson) is a book on crime.